TO THE HILT

TO THE HILT

Coaching Character for Life

KEVIN TEMPLETON

Illustrated by
Andrea McGuirt and Carrie Cook

Two Harbors Press
Minneapolis, MN

Two Harbors Press
322 First Avenue N, 5th floor
Minneapolis, MN 55401
612.455.2293
www.TwoHarborsPress.com

ISBN-13: 978-1-63413-330-2
LCCN: 2015900910

Distributed by Itasca Books

Book Design by Sophie Chi
Scripture quotations are taken from the King James Version of the Bible (Public Domain).
Cover photo: iStockphoto
Interior illustrations: Andrea McGuirt & Carrie Cook
Back Cover photo: Axel Arzola

Printed in the United States of America

CONTENTS

FOREWORD

I have personally known Coach T. for more than thirty years, and I am personally ecstatic about this book! I know few men who care more about the youth of this world. He is a valiant warrior of Jesus Christ. Make no mistake about it, this book is for our good and God's glory. Coach T. is one of the fiercest competitors I have ever met, who deeply loves his family, friends, and players. Coach T. coaches winners. He has coached numerous collegiate All-Americans and led several teams at the high school and collegiate levels to state or national titles.

To the Hilt is about complete character, absolute surrender, and the utmost faithfulness to God and men. It is a practical, applicable, and well-written book. Coach T. uses his incredible storytelling abilities to inspire us to be all-in. Most of us sell ourselves short, don't hit our assignment, quit when the going gets tough, and keep falling into a pattern of making the wrong decisions. The consequences of falling short are enough to not only to destroy a person's life, but also to devastate the lives of those around us. This book is meant to inspire us to be champions and overcomers in our everyday lives.

The decisions you make every day, the friends that you choose, and the disciplines you have are going to make or break you. It's time to realize that your life matters. I encourage you to read this book with an open mind and humble heart. God wants to use you for great things! Are you ready for the fight? Coach T. will show you how to avoid making some of life's most critical mistakes and encourage you to keep making the right decisions. This book captures the timeless truths of God's word that will guide you to a life of no regrets. It's time to be Semper Fi (always faithful). Few books really have the potential to change lives, but this book has the potential to change the world. *To the hilt!*

Buck Sutton
President of Teens for Christ (Lima, Ohio)
(teens-for-christ.com)

ACKNOWLEDGMENTS

I t's been said if you see a turtle on a fence post you know for sure he didn't get there by himself. That's certainly true in my case. I had a lot of help along the way.

The American Heritage Dictionary says acknowledgment is a noun meaning "an expression of thanks or a token of appreciation." So here goes:

Thanks to all our former players over the past thirty-five years. Banners, rings, wins, and awards are nice, but "living trophies" are what really matter. Seeing so many of our former players accomplish so much after their playing careers ended is the most gratifying thing any coach could hope for.

Thanks to our children and grandchildren, who bring enormous joy to our lives every day. No one could be more proud of their children than we are.

Thanks to my parents, Guy and Carol, for their love, guidance, support, and faithful example through the years. I have always held coaches in high esteem, and they are still the best coaches I've ever seen.

TO VICKY:
Doting Nana
Beloved Mother
Precious Gift.

I've followed sports for more than fifty years, but I've never seen a game changer that could even compare to you. What a gift you are … every day.

Most important, I am thankful to God, who has blessed me beyond measure. I praise Him for all He has done and will continue to do as I try to impact others. If we do anything that blesses or encourages other people, "To God be the glory, great things He hath done."

LET'S GET STARTED

Welcome! This book is written for young people, young adults, and the people who care about them. This book can guide you, be a refresher course for you, or serve as a resource as you help others.

You are often bombarded with misinformation about what is right and wrong. You may wonder:

- What makes a person successful?
- How can I be happy?
- What is my purpose in life?

Here's a quick key: get off to a good start.

When a carpenter builds a house, special attention is given to the foundation. If a mistake is made or a shortcut is taken in this initial stage, the house can be deeply flawed. When the foundation is solid, the construction follows naturally.

As a young person, you are laying the foundation for the rest of your life. As an adult, you are building upon that foundation.

> "The foundation stones for a balanced success are honesty, character, integrity, faith, love, and loyalty." —Zig Ziglar

This is good advice. Do you have a balanced outlook on life? Base your life on these foundational stones, and you will avoid many potential problems that can derail your future.

I have more than thirty-five years of experience connecting with teenagers and college students. I love and believe in them. You don't need to be preached at. I have no desire to talk down to you. I'd like to talk to you as a trusted friend or mentor. Everybody needs a mentor to help guide them through the minefields of life. A mentor is someone who sees your potential and believes in you more than you believe in yourself.

I'd love for this book to be a spark that helps you set a solid foundation for your life by helping you develop good habits and establish strong friendships. It will help you streamline your decision making. We all need to be reminded that knowing things is important, but actually following through on what we know is crucial to our success.

I'm a storyteller. I think that's the best way to help folks remember a lesson. My writing is conversational and folksy. It is not deep, nor is it intended to be. We won't be splitting the atom or solving the problems of the Middle East.

Some of these chapters will uplift and inspire you. Some will make you laugh, and some provide a serious warning. Some chapters will force you to examine yourself. Others are designed to make you think.

> **Ready. Set. Read! Let's find out**
> **how to live life to the hilt!**

TO THE HILT

"Good players buy in. Great players are locked in.
Champions are all in."
—Tom Crean, Indiana University

"Whatsoever thy hand findeth to do,
do it with thy might . . ."
—Ecclesiastes 9:10

P icture yourself on the battlefield in a *Braveheart*-type setting. You are fighting for family, home, and freedom. Your way of life and your own existence depend on the outcome of that battle.

How would you fight?

Do you think you would daintily stick your enemy?

Would you stick him a couple of inches deep in the shoulder to try to convince him to go home and leave you alone? Not me! I've never been called on to go to a battlefield and fight to defend the ones I love. (Maybe that's why I have so much respect for those who have made great sacrifices to keep our country free.) But I can only imagine that any enemy that threatens my family is going to face all the force that I can bring to the battlefield. There would be no half measures. I wouldn't stick or stab them. I'd run them all the way through—*to the hilt.*

John Stuart Mill said, "One person with a belief is equal to a force of ninety-nine who have only interests." He was close, but the truth is one person with commitment is a greater force than ninety-nine who have only interests. Passion, enthusiasm, conviction, fire in your belly—call it what you will—ensures that a person won't take no for an answer. There are no plan B contingencies.

Do you know what it means to live your life to the hilt? According to Webster's dictionary, this phrase means "to the very limit" or "completely." For example, "The business was mortgaged to the hilt." A second definition is "with nothing lacking," such as "She played the point guard role to the hilt."

The word *hilt* is a noun referring to a part of a sword or dagger. A sword has three parts. Most people can only name two of them: the handle and the blade. You cut things with the blade. You hold the sword with the handle. When you are on the battlefield, your hands would get sweaty. The blood would also tend to make the handle very slippery. (If things are going well during battle, there will be some involuntary blood donors on the other side.) If you were dealing with an extremely sharp sword in the heat of battle, you would need something to prevent your hand from slipping. The part of the sword that protects your hand from the blade is the hilt.

> **Three things keep us from living life to the hilt.**
> 1. Our standards are too low.
> 2. We fear failure.
> 3. We have a lack of commitment.

The first is that we don't have high enough standards. We are satisfied with pretty good, not that bad, better than some, or better than George. Hey, you can always find somebody you're better than. That's not a very high standard. If my standard is to be an above-average husband or a better husband than the drunk who lives down the street who beats his wife, that is not a very high standard. We should have high standards in our lives. Our standard should be to become the best son or daughter, the best brother or sister, the best neighbor, the best employee, the best church member, and so on. I don't want to be a C+ husband or a C+ teacher or a C+ grandfather. So what I'm saying is: let's raise our standards so we can be the best that we are capable of being.

Girls, raise your standards for the guy you would be interested in dating. It should be that he is a great guy, not that he doesn't treat you as badly as your previous boyfriend. Don't settle for above average. Be on the lookout for a guy who is the best and treats you the way you deserve to be treated—with respect. The same goes for guys—wait for the best. A girl with character, inner beauty, and a good sense of humor who is kind to others is far more desirable than a self-absorbed, high-maintenance drama queen.

The next thing that keeps us from living life to the hilt is fear of failure. Don't be afraid to be criticized by people who are sitting in the stands. They don't have the guts to go for it themselves, but they want to criticize other people who are willing to risk failure in order to succeed. Many times the greatest rewards go to those who are willing to take the greatest risks. Don't let pride, fear of embarrassment, and failure hold you back.

The final thing that keeps us from living life to the hilt is a lack of commitment. There's a big difference between being committed and being interested. When we are interested in something, we do it when it is convenient. We do it when it works into our schedule. When you are committed to something, it is a priority regardless of how difficult it is or how inconvenient it is. You have a laser-like focus to reach your goal.

Hernando Cortez was a Spanish conquistador who went to Mexico in 1519. Cortez had six hundred soldiers and eleven ships. He introduced horses to a new continent. Many other conquerors with superior resources had attempted to colonize the Yucatan Peninsula without success. The powerful Aztecs ruled the central valley of Mexico with a mighty empire that plundered weaker tribes and hoarded vast amounts of gold, silver, and jewelry. The Aztecs were feared and hated by the other tribes. Cortez needed a way to energize and motivate his men.

After landing, Cortez's men were probably more than a little fearful and nervous about the unknown challenges they might face in this new land. The men expected their leader to inspire and reassure them that their mission would be a success. Visions of riches no doubt danced in their heads. They were eager to hear Cortez's instructions.

The first thing Cortez told the men was, "Burn the boats. All of them." Would you have done that? Not me! I'd keep one ship just in case the enemies were too tough. The Spaniards had gunpowder weapons, but what if the Aztecs had lasers? What if there were monsters/dinosaurs/zombies/diseases that were too numerous or difficult to deal with? Hey, the unknown can be a very frightening prospect.

Cortez answered his crew's fears and maybe his own doubts by burning all the ships. It was his way of pushing all his chips into the center of the table. They were all-in. They were committed to the mission and to each other. They would be wildly successful or die in the attempt. We could say that Cortez lived to the hilt. Defeat was never an option.

> **Let's dream big dreams for God to use us in ways we hardly thought possible.**

God doesn't discourage our ambitions as long as we use our success as a platform to spread His Word and glorify Him.

Are you living to the hilt at home, at school, at church, in the neighborhood, on your team, or wherever you are? If you're not, raise your standards to excellence. Stop settling for just getting by. Don't worry about what anybody else thinks. *Live life to the hilt every day!*

DISCUSSION QUESTIONS

1. What does living "to the hilt" mean to you today?
    - At home?
    - At school?
    - At work?
    - In your daily walk with Christ?

2. What are the advantages of living to the hilt?

3. What are some disadvantages of living to the hilt?

4. What are some costs of refusing to live to the hilt?

BIBLE PASSAGES FOR ADDITIONAL STUDY

I Kings 17:9–16

John 6:8–13

TAKE TOTAL RESPONSIBILITY

"Eventually we all have to accept full and total
responsibility for our actions, everything we have done,
and have not done."

—Hubert Selby Jr.

"The woman *which thou gavest* to be with me . . ."

—Genesis 8:12

W hen was the last time you made an excuse for
yourself?

When was the last time you blamed someone
else for a problem you had or a condition that you faced?

How long has it been since you complained about
something?

For most of us the habits of excuses, blaming others,
and complaining occur far too often. If some people spent
the energy completing unfinished projects that they use to

explain away their lack of progress, they would amaze people, probably even themselves, with their achievements.

Excuses, explanations, whining, and blaming others are not part of the recipe for success. They are signs of immaturity. We need to be brutally honest with ourselves.

Maturity is not an age. There are some ages that are accepted as stepping stones to maturity. For example, you have to be at least thirty-five years of age to be eligible to be the President of the United States. You can vote when you turn eighteen years of age. But maturity is not a set age. I have had many young people in my classes who were fourteen and very mature. Some people are forty and very immature. This is sad to say, but some people never grow up.

Some characteristics of a mature person are:

- Being willing to sacrifice personal convenience for the welfare of others. Certainly, anyone who is not willing to sacrifice their own personal convenience should never have children. Children are needy. They are extremely selfish. It takes an immense amount of time, patience, money, and energy to parent a child effectively.

- Being able to suffer an injustice without having to get even with the person who was responsible for your pain. Do you have to get even? Can you just let it go?

- Being able to finish a difficult job without constant supervision. Anybody can start a job, but can you finish it? Anybody can work diligently while being closely supervised. What if the boss isn't around?

forgive people →

finish things, don't give up

patience

- Being able to have money in your pocket without having to spend it. It is fun to spend money. It is fun to get instant gratification. It's difficult to keep the big picture in mind and delay the rewards that come with responsibility and patience.

> **The biggest step to being a mature individual is when you take total responsibility for yourself.**

This is not something that is easy to do. It just seems natural for us to make excuses, blame someone else, whine about difficulties, and complain when things don't go the way we had planned. A responsible person doesn't make excuses. He accepts responsibility and works to improve things that are not up to par. He isn't looking for a scapegoat to blame when things get a little sideways. He already knows life is not fair and can be extremely difficult at times. He accepts that challenges are inevitable. An immature person complains, moans, and whines. I recently had a fellow teacher complaining for a good ten minutes about not having enough time to get a task done. All that did was rob him and put him ten minutes further behind. Does that make any sense to you?

Nobody wants to hear an adult whining like a little two-year-old anyway. Let's face it: all of us have challenges and difficulties. I am an old grandpa. I am fifty-six years old and they give me a class of kids who are fourteen years old. I'm a diabetic. Sometimes my blood sugar will spike very high. This makes it very difficult for me to think and speak clearly.

Other times my blood sugar level can drop dangerously low. These are very real issues, which I have to manage carefully. But none of these factors are suitable excuses for me to do a poor job of teaching my classes.

My boss doesn't care about my age. He doesn't care about how energetic my students are. My boss doesn't care about my diabetic condition. He doesn't want to hear explanations and excuses. He just wants to know if I can do the job. Will I show up every day, on time and prepared for class? Do I care about the kids? Can I reach, teach, and motivate young people? If I can't connect with young people, or if I am not passionate about the call to teach, then my boss will want to get somebody in that classroom who can do those things. He isn't interested in hearing how tough it is to regulate my blood sugar level. He doesn't care about my diet concerns. He just wants to get results and know that I am on target in the classroom.

Unfortunately, wanting to shirk responsibility is as old as the Garden of Eden. Adam was given the responsibility to rule over creation (Genesis 1:27–29). There was only one tree he wasn't to eat from. We know Adam didn't take responsibility for his sin. He blamed Eve and ultimately God himself (Genesis 3:8–12). Eve blamed the serpent. And the tradition carries on until today. We still don't want to face up to our responsibilities. Our excuses are just as lame as Adam and Eve's.

There are no excuses that can explain away and justify our irresponsible actions. If you are not happy with:

- Your grades—study harder, get serious, and find a tutor.

- Your fitness level—hit the gym and exercise.
- Your relationships—work harder at them. Invest more time, and be more thoughtful and kind.
- Your spiritual condition—set aside time to pray and read your Bible.
- Your job—find one that suits your needs better, or maybe even make a career change that will increase your job satisfaction.
- Your debts—stop spending. Be satisfied with what you have.
- Your attitude—change it. Start every day with a positive attitude.

> "Happiness isn't about getting what you want all the time. It is about loving what you have and being grateful for it." —Zig Ziglar

When I coach a team, I want them to avoid being selfish, shady, and soft. Their focus needs to be on the team. Selfish guys care about their stats, their playing time, or their gratification. They need to be trustworthy. No excuses or explanations. We can trust them to do the right thing at home, in the classroom, and on the court during practice or in a game. All team members need to be tough. No explanations or excuses, just total responsibility. Soft people always have an explanation. They will get us a loss.

You might come from a single-parent home. That's hard. You might be ADHD. You might live in a rough neighborhood. These are tough obstacles, but they can't be overcome with excuses and blame. Take responsibility for your life. This is a much better option than playing the "I'm too young," "I'm a girl," "I'm a minority," "I'm from a single-parent home," "I'm a diabetic," "I'm from a rough background," or "I have OCD" cards.

If you face some of the hardships mentioned in the above paragraph, the answer is to refuse to play any of the victim cards. Turn to an adult that you trust. Get some help from a teacher, a coach, your youth pastor, or an aunt or uncle. You have to be proactive. You be the one to reach out and take the first step.

Think of life as being a huge staircase with success sitting all the way at the top. You will take a giant leap toward being successful if you take total responsibility for yourself.

If you choose the "I'm a victim. Boo hoo! Poor little me" card, you only give yourself a much higher climb to success.

DISCUSSION QUESTIONS

1. Why is it hard to take total responsibility for yourself?

2. What are the benefits of taking total responsibility?

3. What are the costs of shirking your responsibility?

4. How can you take responsibility for your spiritual condition (see James 4:8)?

5. Are any of my excuses as ridiculous as Aaron's? (see Exodus 32)

BIBLE PASSAGES FOR ADDITIONAL STUDY

Exodus 32:19–24
1 Samuel 15:3, 9, 13–15

WHAT KIND OF SOLDIER ARE YOU?

"The soldier is summoned to a life of active duty
and so is the Christian."
—William Gurnall

"…endure hardness as a good soldier of Jesus Christ."
—II Timothy 2:3

In writing to Timothy, the apostle Paul tells him to "endure hardness as a good soldier of Jesus Christ." The life of a soldier is full of danger, hardship, uncertainty, and sacrifice. The soft need not apply. The soft would quit. They couldn't endure the hardness. Since Paul tells Timothy to be a good soldier, it stands to reason that some soldiers are better than others—and not all soldiers are good. Some are average, and others are poor/substandard.

In the United States we have had many famous soldiers. Some even rode their battlefield glory all the way to the White House.

What kind of soldier are you?

How would you measure up to great warriors of US history?

Before you answer, let me tell you about a couple of soldiers who you may not have heard of before.

In President Reagan's first inaugural address on January 20, 1981, he told us of Martin Treptow. Treptow was a small-town barber in peacetime who enlisted in the Iowa National Guard. He was placed in the Forty-Second Division. It was an infantry division of men from Alabama, Ohio, New York, Wisconsin, and Iowa. It was called the Rainbow Division because the men were from all over the country. This division fought with distinction on many battlefields.

In July 1918 the Forty-Second Division engaged the Germans at the Second Battle of the Marne. During that battle Treptow carried a message between battalions under heavy artillery fire. He was hit and killed, but the message got through.

When they bundled up Treptow's belongings to send to his family back home, they found his journal. On the flyleaf under the heading "My Pledge," Treptow had written:

> "America must win this war. Therefore, I will work, I will save, I will sacrifice, I will endure, I will fight cheerfully and do my utmost, *as if the issue of the whole struggle depended on me alone.*"

What if everybody in your church was exactly like you? What would the attendance be like?

What if everybody on your team gave the same amount of effort in practice as you do?

What if everybody in your class was exactly as teachable as you are?

What if everyone in your family was exactly as unselfish, as kind, and as thoughtful as you are? What would your home be like?

What if everyone was as generous to volunteer their time or donate money for needy charities as you are?

What if everyone at work was as dependable as you, got along with their coworkers like you, or worked as hard as you?

Obviously, as Christians our struggles are not entirely up to us. We have divine help. We should pray for God to help us while working "as if the whole struggle depended on us alone."

Another soldier who I read about recently was Lance Corporal Jeffrey Nashton. On October 23, 1983, a Mercedes truck loaded with 12,000 pounds of TNT crashed into an aviation building at the Beirut International Airport. The Eighth Marine Battalion used this location as their barracks. It was a dark day in Marine Corps history, as 241 marines were killed and another 112 were wounded.

General Paul Kelley rushed to visit his wounded marines, who had been taken to a hospital in Wiesbaden, Germany. When Kelley visited, Nashton was in critical condition. He was unable to speak and had been temporarily blinded by the dust off the concrete blocks. One officer said Nashton had "more tubes going in and out of his body than I have ever seen." Nashton suffered a fractured skull, a smashed right cheekbone, seven broken ribs, a broken leg, and a severely bruised heart. His lungs also collapsed. He had no memory of the two days between the explosion and General Kelley's arrival.

When told that the commandant of the Marine Corps had come to visit him, Nashton didn't really believe it. He couldn't see and he couldn't speak. He reached up to touch the stars on the shoulder of General Kelley's uniform. He counted one, two, three, *four* stars! When he realized it really was General Kelley, he tried to write with his finger on the bed sheet. No one could decipher what he was trying to say. After they brought Nashton a pad of paper and a pencil, he wrote "Semper Fi." His note brought the commandant and a room full of combat-hardened marines to tears.

Semper Fi is marine shorthand for *semper fidelis*, a Latin phrase meaning "always faithful." He was trying to say, "You can count on me. I will always do my job. Don't worry about me. I'll be at my post, serving my country." This story inspires me every time I think about it. Nashton returned to active duty in early January 1984, just a little more than two months after the explosion. *Semper Fi.*

The question for us to consider is this:

What kind of Christian am I?

- Draft Dodger—I haven't become a Christian yet.
- Missing in Action—I'm a Christian, but I'm not actively in the battle every day.

- Prisoner of War—I fell into Satan's trap.
- Wounded—I used to be actively involved in prayer, Bible reading, witnessing, etc., but I got hurt and left the battlefield.
- Semper Fi—I've taken some hits, but I want to serve God and be faithful to Him.

We need all available soldiers on the battlefield. Our enemy is invisible but just as real as any enemy we could face on the field of battle.

Reach out to the draft dodgers. Help them enlist on the winning side.

Reach out to the MIAs, POWs, and wounded soldiers. They need a hand and a word of encouragement, not a judgmental attitude.

> **Let's ask God to help us be Semper Fi Christians for His glory.**

DISCUSSION QUESTIONS

1. Would you consider military service? Why? Why not?

2. What kind of soldier would you be right now?

3. How can you endure hardness as a good soldier?

4. What role does commitment play in your life as a Christian?

BIBLE PASSAGES FOR ADDITIONAL STUDY

II Timothy 2:3–4
Ephesians 6:11–18

CHOICES AND CONSEQUENCES

"You write your life story by the choices you make.
Those moments of decision are so difficult."
—Helen Mirren

"Choose you this day whom you will serve . . ."
—Joshua 24:15

I recently read that the average American makes about thirty-five thousand decisions daily. Most of them are simple:

- Blue shirt or green shirt?
- Solid shirt or striped shirt?
- Frosted Flakes or Cap'n Crunch?
- Right lane or left lane?
- Wait to pull out into traffic or go for it?
- Turn on blinker or eh?
- Sit up front or sit in the middle?

- Tacos or pizza for lunch?
- Three tacos or four tacos?
- Answer the phone or call back later?
- Go for the green or play a safe layup?

Other decisions are more important:

- How hard am I willing to work for a good education?
- Where will I go to school? What will I major in?
- What job will I take? How hard will I work?
- Am I going to date? What type of person will I date?
- What will I do on a date? What will I not do on a date?
- Am I going to get married? What type of person will I marry?
- How seriously will I take my marriage?
- Will we have kids? How many? How will we raise those kids?
- Will I go to church? Where? How often?

There are consequences to the choices we make. If you skip breakfast, you might get really hungry before you have lunch. If you get up late, you might have to rush to get to work on time. If you are in a rush to get to work, you might drive recklessly or exceed the speed limit. If you exceed the speed limit, you might get pulled over and get a ticket. Or you might not.

We get to make choices, but we don't get to choose the consequences. The best way I can think of to illustrate this fact is to tell you about the best high school football player I ever saw play in person, Adarius Bowman.

I love to watch sports. High school sports, college sports, professional sports, it really doesn't matter. I especially like football and basketball. These sports are fast-paced. The crowd can really get involved in the game. I have seen a lot of extremely talented athletes play high school football in my lifetime.

The first athlete I was overwhelmed by was James Brooks. Brooks wasn't big, but he was a powerful runner and return man. He played for Warner-Robbins High School and he totally destroyed a defending state champion Baylor (Chattanooga, Tennessee) team when he was a senior. He went on to a stellar career at Auburn, where he earned All-American status. He set school records for kickoff return yards and all-purpose yards (5,596) while scoring thirty touchdowns. Brooks played twelve years in the NFL and was a four-time Pro Bowler.

The second-most-memorable high school footballer was Cris Carter. I saw him dominate Lima Senior High School (Lima, Ohio) while playing for Middletown High School. He was also amazing on the basketball court for the Middies. He went on to star at Ohio State with a Rose Bowl–record nine receptions for 172 yards as a freshman. He set the Ohio State record with 168 career receptions in three years. He secretly signed with an agent after his junior season. When the contract was revealed, Carter was ruled ineligible for the 1987 season. Ohio State struggled to a 6–4–1 record and Coach Earle Bruce was fired.

Carter was an eight-time Pro Bowler, and he caught 1,101 passes for 130 touchdowns in the NFL. He was elected to the Pro Football Hall of Fame on February 2, 2013.

While James Brooks and Cris Carter were amazing on the football field, I still say the best high school player I ever saw in person was Adarius Bowman. We actually went to see the other team play that night. Bowman's very pedestrian Notre Dame team almost knocked off the mighty Blue Tornado of McCallie, who went on to win the TSSAA AAA State Championship. As a junior wide receiver in that 2001 game, Bowman had 293 receiving yards and five touchdowns in a losing effort. He was covered by three and four players, yet he still would rise above the crowd and make spectacular catches. He played in the 2003 US Army All-American Bowl, a game that features the top players in the country.

At six feet three inches and 220 pounds, Bowman was recruited by virtually every top football college in the entire country. He enrolled at UNC and played two seasons before being released from the team for possession of marijuana.

He transferred to Oklahoma State and sat out the 2005 season as a redshirt. He had a terrific junior season, highlighted by a performance against Kansas that led to him being the National Player of the Week. He had thirteen receptions for three hundred yards and four touchdowns. After the season Bowman was the Big Twelve Conference Newcomer of the Year and the Oklahoma State MVP.

Going into the 2007 season Bowman was considered the nineteenth best senior prospect by draft guru Mel Kiper Jr. His senior season was a little disappointing with sixty-one catches,

932 yards, and seven touchdowns, but he was still considered a mid-to-late second-round NFL selection. Todd McShay, ESPN draft analyst, felt Bowman would have gone at the end of the first round until he ran an uncharacteristically slow 4.74 forty-yard dash at the NFL combine.

On April 1, 2008, Bowman was arrested in Athens, Tennessee, for possession of marijuana. It was only days before the NFL Draft. Bowman went undrafted. He started the season as the number nineteen prospect and saw more than 200 players selected without his name being called. McShay called the fall unprecedented and noted that second-round draft pick average contracts are for four years and $8 million. Entering his senior season he was the top prospect in the Big Twelve Conference (Texas, Oklahoma, Texas Tech, Baylor, etc.). What a shame!

Adarius Bowman had speed, agility, size, strength, great hands, and amazing leaping ability. He was given gifts by God that very few people possess. But he made a bad choice. He rehabilitated himself, but then he made more bad choices. The final choice led to his arrest. He was ashamed. He hurt his family. He cost himself an opportunity very few collegiate players get: a chance for NFL stardom. For what? Weed? Wow, he possessed an $8 million joint.

No NFL team offered Bowman a contract. He played a year in the CFL with the Saskatchewan Roughriders in 2008. He was traded to the Winnipeg Blue Bombers in April 2009. He had 925 receiving yards and six touchdowns. He dropped a lot of passes in the 2010 season and was cut in October 2010. Bowman had a good season for the Edmonton Eskimos in

2011, but his 2012 season ended in the second game of the season when he tore his ACL and MCL in his left knee.

You get to make choices every day. Some aren't that big of a deal; some choices are really big.

- Will you try drugs? Alcohol? Tobacco products?
- Will you become sexually active before marriage?
- Will you cheat on a test?
- Will you lie to try to get out of a jam?
- Will you take something that doesn't belong to you if no one is looking?
- Will you quit school?
- Will you do what you know in your heart is the right thing when you are pressured to do something that is highly questionable?
- Will you do what you know is right when the majority isn't?
- Will you be faithful to your spouse?

> **Be careful to think things through and make good choices.**
> **You get to make choices, but you don't get to choose the consequences.**

DISCUSSION QUESTIONS

1. What are some important decisions you will have to make today?

2. What are some important decisions you will make in the next two years?

3. Who would you go to for advice about a crucial decision?

4. How should you make important decisions?

BIBLE PASSAGE FOR ADDITIONAL STUDY

Genesis 13:5–13

YOU MAKE YOUR CHOICES

"We almost always have choices,
and the better the choice,
the more we will be in control of our lives."
—William Glassner

"Be not deceived; God is not mocked:
for whatsoever a man soweth, that shall he also reap."
—Galatians 6:7

A terrible accident happened to a young fellow who lives just a few miles from our house. He was a high school sophomore from Signal Mountain, Tennessee, named David Anderson III. David was involved in a lot of activities in high school, and he played on the baseball team.

He was hanging out with friends in late August 2010. They had been bouncing on a trampoline and later swimming in an above-ground pool. If you know anything about above-ground pools, you know that they are covered with stickers that warn you it is dangerous to dive into these pools. The week before, David was diving into one, so he didn't think much about it. He was a fun guy. He moved the trampoline over, jumped, and dove into the pool.

After his head hit the bottom of the pool, David couldn't get out. He dislocated two vertebrae in his neck. At first his friends thought he was clowning around. Then they realized he was hurt and in serious trouble. They jumped in and pulled him out of the water. After a frantic 911 call, David was taken to Erlanger Hospital in Chattanooga, Tennessee. A metal plate was implanted in his back. A few days later, David was taken to the Shepherd Center, a brain and spinal cord rehabilitation facility in Atlanta.

David spent the next three months at the Shepherd Center. He was left partially paralyzed. He returned home the day before Thanksgiving. "It's a different life now. When you wake up, it takes a good hour and a half to two hours to eat breakfast and get dressed," he told Michael Stone of the *Chattanooga Times Free Press*. His mom, Rhonda, added, "It's like being an infant and starting all over."

Just take a few moments and absorb that last paragraph. *Two hours* to eat breakfast and get dressed? Being an infant—starting over? No thanks. And that's after progressing through rehab, to go from only being able to shrug his shoulders to being able to move his head, wrists, and left arm. Eating, brushing your teeth, and getting dressed being major accomplishments? Wow! Former pro football player Alex Karras was right when he said, "Toughness is in your soul, not in your muscles."

David was not a bad guy. Everybody enjoyed hanging out with him. He didn't commit a crime. He just made a foolish choice to get a laugh. The consequences are still devastating years later.

Let me illustrate this in another way. Ten years ago, Justin Verlander was the second baseball player selected in the Major League Baseball Draft. He pitched three years at Old Dominion in Richmond, Virginia. He set practically every school and conference pitching record as he averaged 11.5 strikeouts per nine innings pitched for his career.

Verlander has established himself as the best pitcher in baseball. He was the American League (AL) Rookie of the Year in 2006. A six-time All-Star, Verlander won the AL MVP in 2011. He had led the AL in strikeouts three times (2009, 2011, and 2012), pitched two no-hitters, and pitched in the World Series twice (2007 and 2011).

In late March 2013, Verlander agreed to a base contract of $20 million in 2013 and 2014, and $28 million a year through 2019. He and the team have an option year in 2020 for $22 million. The $202 million deal made Verlander the highest-paid pitcher in Major League Baseball at the time.

All this information about Verlander makes you wonder: Who was the top pick? Who did the Padres draft in 2004 ahead of Verlander, and is that player in uniform today?

Matt Bush was the overall number one pick in the 2004 baseball draft as an eighteen-year-old high school shortstop. He was a hometown hero for Mission Bay High School, which is located just ten miles from Petco Park, where the San Diego Padres play their home games. Bush could do it all on a baseball diamond. Scouts look for players with five skills (ability to run, throw, catch, hit for power, and hit for average). Matt's talents allowed him to go from sitting in English class to being swarmed by news trucks wanting to interview the baseball phenom.

It is now ten years later, and Matt Bush isn't a kid anymore. He is still found wearing a uniform every day. Matt isn't on the field anymore. He is serving time at the Hamilton Correctional Institution in Jasper, Florida, close to the Georgia line. Bush no doubt dreamt of being in uniform, but it is doubtful that he ever saw himself in an orange jumpsuit. The number on his back is DC#07392.

Bush spent eight years with three different minor league teams. Bush underachieved in the minor leagues as he quickly developed an alcohol problem.

In March 2012 Matt Bush borrowed roommate Brandon Guyer's truck "to run some errands" on a day off. His teammate had no clue that Bush's driver's license had been revoked for previous DUI convictions.

While on his way to the Verizon store, Bush decided to have one beer. The gas station sold a huge alcoholic energy drink called Four Loko. He drank it quickly and stopped numerous times for another drink on the forty-five-minute drive to the mall.

Eventually, he sideswiped a utility pole with the side of Guyer's vehicle. He should have known to stop driving at that point. Unfortunately, he kept going.

Bush told Gabe Kapler of Fox Sports, "The right side of Brandon's car was dented in really bad. Man, it felt so awful that I had to bring him back his brand-new truck [in this condition]. I was really, really scared to bring him back his car that way."

Instead of stopping, Bush was speeding and driving in a reckless manner. He passed numerous cars before hitting the back tire of Tony Tufano's motorcycle. Tufano's bike went out from under him. Bush took off in the Durango after the accident and ran over Tufano's head with a back tire. He panicked and just kept going. Bush was eventually pulled over by police. He had a blood alcohol level of .18 (.08 is considered driving while intoxicated in Florida). Tufano, seventy-four, was in a coma and had a collapsed lung and several broken bones. Tufano still doesn't remember the crash.

Bush pled no contest to driving under the influence with serious bodily injury. He was sentenced to fifty-one months in prison. He will get out of prison in May 2016.

Tufano's family sued both Bush and Guyer for $5 million in a civil suit. The suit was settled out of court for an undisclosed amount. His lawyers are considering a suit against Bush's team, the Rays, because they knew Bush had an alcohol problem. The Rays knew he had two previous DUI convictions that had caused the Padres and the Blue Jays to release him.

Bush's undeniable physical tools were trumped by poor decision-making and addiction. "I want people to know that I'm very sorry for what occurred," he said. "I really wish things had been a lot different. I would've made a lot better choices."

I realize it is a little depressing to read the stories about David and Matt Bush. The point is that we have to realize our choices will play a crucial part in our future. If we make good decisions, we will get better results. If we make poor decisions, the results could be catastrophic.

When my buddies and I play golf, we sometimes hit a poor tee shot on the first hole. We then take a mulligan. A mulligan is a do-over. We don't count the first shot. We just play it from there and go on. We aren't professionals.

> There aren't any mulligans in life.
> We make our choices, and then our choices make us.

DISCUSSION QUESTIONS

1. What would be some choices that keep you safe in the future?

2. How would choosing to be a witness to others affect your life?

3. What are some good choices that you have made that positively affected your life?

4. How can you pick up the pieces after making a bad choice?

BIBLE PASSAGE FOR ADDITIONAL STUDY

Ecclesiastes 10:1

IF YOU LIVE FOR THE MOMENT...

"Before you make a decision, ask yourself:
will you regret the results or rejoice in them?"
—Rob Liano

"Esau, who for one morsel of meat
sold his birthright . . .
for he found no place of repentance,
though he sought it carefully with tears."
—Hebrews 12:16, 17

Bobby Phills was an outstanding professional basketball player for the Charlotte franchise in the NBA. Bobby was respected by his teammates and his opponents and was active in the community. He volunteered for children's charities and was a finalist for the NBA's Sportsmanship Award. He started the Bobby Phills Educational Foundation. "He was such a special person.

He could have been one of the foremost black leaders in the country. He had the brainpower. He had the great family background, he had everything," said Ben Jobe, Phills's former coach at Southern University. "Bobby was just a treasure to be around," according to Clay Mosher, an assistant coach when Phills played for the CBA's Sioux Falls Sky Force. Southern University chancellor Edward R. Jackson said, "We are deeply saddened by the tragic loss of this outstanding human being. This young man represented the very best of Southern University. He was not only a world-class athlete, but also a world-class humanitarian."

Cleveland Cavaliers president Wayne Embry gave Phills his start in the NBA. "Bobby Phills was all that you would want in a human being. He had extremely high character. He was a family man. I can't tell you what he meant to the Cavaliers. If there's a person you would want to be a role model for your children, it's Bobby Phills." NBA commissioner David Stern said Phills "was a caring member of the community."

On Wednesday, January 12, 2000, Bobby Phills was killed when he was racing with teammate David Wesley. He was driving at more than 75 miles an hour when he lost control of the 1997 Porsche 993 Cabriolet and skidded into oncoming traffic. Charlotte police spokesman Keith Bridges said "it looked like they were drag racing." Phills, thirty years old, was leaving a team practice at the Charlotte Coliseum about eleven a.m. when he lost control of his car and was killed instantly. He was less than a mile from the arena.

Stunned and tearful, teammates and team officials gathered at the accident scene. Just minutes earlier, Phills and the other players had been practicing for Wednesday night's game with the Chicago Bulls.

A police crash investigator said Phills lost control of his Porsche on a dangerous curve where the posted speed was 45 miles per hour. "The skid marks indicate he was not going in a straight line," said Captain L. E. Blydenburgh. Phills's 1997 convertible with a vanity license plate—*SLAMN*— left skid marks several hundred feet long and came to rest in one of the opposite lanes.

Bobby Phills was a six foot five defensive stopper, but he could score as well. He would play much like Luol Deng of the Heat or Metta World Peace, if World Peace had any sense. He often started at shooting guard or small forward. He was considered one of the team leaders. He joined the Hornets in 1997 after six years in Cleveland and was in the third year of a seven-year, $33 million contract. He averaged eleven points, 3.2 rebounds, and 2.7 assists for his career. "He touched all of our lives," said Bob Bass, the Hornets' executive vice president of basketball operations. "It's shocking."

Bobby Phills and his wife have two children—Bobby Ray III, three, and Kerstie, one. "This is the ultimate tragedy. Our immediate thoughts and prayers are with his wife, Kendall, their children and family," Hornets owner George Shinn said in a statement. "Not only was Bobby a tremendous person, but a great husband, father, and role model that everyone respected and admired. He was someone you would want your children to be like."

Life lesson number six is very simple. *If you live for the moment, the moment will pass, and you will regret it.*

Bobby Phills was a good guy. He was respected and he was loved. He was generous. He cared about other people and was very active in his community. Bobby made a terrible decision, and that decision cost him his life. What a shame! We will never know all that he could've accomplished if he had not made that fatal choice.

Bobby was from a good family. His father, Dr. Bobby Phills, is the director of the College of Engineering Sciences, Technology, and Agriculture at Florida A&M University. It doesn't matter how good your family is or if you are a college graduate. You still have to make good choices.

It is a shame that Bobby Phills will be remembered not for what he accomplished, but for what might have been. He had a fast car, he raced with his friend, and it cost him not only his life but his legacy. He lived for the moment, the moment passed, and many people regretted that decision.

I had a girl in class a few years ago. We will call her Z. She was very pleasant and she was always the first to get to class. She would greet me every day with a friendly smile. She had a great attitude. She worked very hard in class and earned an A. She was fourteen and a great gal. What a sparkling future she had in front of her! I did not see Z around the school for quite some time after she moved on to the next class. Probably two years after I had her in class, I saw her at a football game. I was taking Elena, our then-two-year-old granddaughter, to the concession stand to get some popcorn. Z came up and greeted us. She was carrying a toddler in her arms. He looked to be about a year and a half or two years old. He was quite a load, probably forty-five pounds or so. I was hoping she would say he was her nephew, but it was not to be. We stepped back from the crowd and she told me her story. She fell hard for an upperclassman. She loved him and he said that he loved her. She felt sure that this was not just "puppy love"; this was the real thing—big dog stuff. Tears were streaming down her face. Her son's father lost interest in her quickly after she got pregnant. He wanted nothing to do with her or their son. I asked if he paid child support, and she said no. I told her she should pursue getting him to support his son, and she said it would just be too painful. He had another girlfriend, and Z couldn't deal with all the awkwardness and hostility.

She said, "I should have listened to you, Coach T. You tried to tell us. You told us to be careful about the choices that we make because they have consequences. You warned us not to live for the moment. That's what I did; I lived for the moment. I thought he loved me. I didn't think he would do what he did. It hurts so bad. How could I be so dumb?" I asked her if she had ever considered giving her son up for adoption. There would be many families who would love to give him a good home. She could give them and her son a great gift. It would help her to have a future and get her education. It was a delicate situation, but I felt I had to ask her if she had considered it. She said she couldn't even consider giving up her son. "He's all I've got." I fully understood. She was in such a tough spot. I am very proud of her for taking responsibility for her son like we talked about back in chapter three.

She's a very smart girl. She would do extremely well in college but will have a difficult time finishing high school. It was very frustrating not to be able to help her. I am afraid the future will be very difficult for her and her son. She lived for the moment and now has to face some very difficult consequences.

I have said all that to say this:

> **If you live for the moment, the moment will pass and you will regret it.**

DISCUSSION QUESTIONS

1. What is a decision you regret making?

2. Were you able to repair the damage of that poor decision?

3. Why is it hard to keep from living for the moment?

4. How can you live with the big picture in mind rather than just living for the moment?

BIBLE PASSAGES FOR ADDITIONAL STUDY

Genesis 25:24–34
Hebrews 12:14–17

SOME THINGS YOU CAN'T PLAY WITH

"Nobody ever did, or ever will,
escape the consequences of his choices."
—Alfred Montapert

"Fools make a mock of sin . . ."
—Proverbs 14:9

H ave you ever been to SeaWorld?
Did you like it?
What did you enjoy the most about your trip to SeaWorld?

Many times you look forward to something, and at the end you're just disappointed because it didn't measure up to your expectations. SeaWorld was not like that for us. We had a great time. We went to SeaWorld while on a family vacation with our children and our grandchildren. They had several rides that we enjoyed. I still remember an outstanding roller coaster called the

Kraaken. It was so fast I lost a pair of sunglasses on that roller coaster. But without a doubt, the highlight of the trip to the park was the show with the animals. They have dolphins that perform and do tricks. Of course, the finale has a huge five-and-a-half-ton killer whale doing various stunts with the trainers.

Daniel Dukes was always fascinated by the killer whales at SeaWorld. He had a strong desire to jump into the tank and play with the whales. He often told his friends that he was going to do just that. He asked them if they wanted to join him. For some reason, none of them wanted anything to do with his plan.

Can you imagine why they did not think it is a good idea to jump in the water with a five-to-six-ton animal?

- The water is kept extremely cold for the whales—about 50 degrees Fahrenheit.
- The animals are wild.
- Most of us don't have any training to deal with these animals.
- They are called killer whales.
- They are not called warm, fuzzy puppy whales. Killer whales.

You don't have to be a Rhodes Scholar to come to the realization that it might not be a great move to jump in the tank and frolic with these creatures. Just a thought!

Daniel didn't have any success convincing his friends to join him on his SeaWorld adventure. He talked about it all the time and finally did something about it. On July 5, 1999, Daniel Dukes went to SeaWorld. It is thought that Daniel hid in a bathroom until after the park closed and then got into the tank with the killer whale. This seems to be the most plausible explanation for how he got the opportunity to do what he did. It is possible but not likely that he broke into the park during the night. At any rate, the next morning the trainers found Daniel's shoes and neatly folded clothing at the side of the pool. The giant five-and-a-half-ton killer whale Tilikum was resting at the side of the pool. Daniel Duke's naked body was lying on the whale's back. He was dead.

An autopsy revealed that Daniel's body was covered with small bite marks on the sides of his arms, legs, and torso. These bites were superficial. The cause of death was drowning. When the twenty-six-year-old jumped into the pool, the whale was surprised. Then the whale got excited because he thought he had a new toy to play with. Daniel's intention was to play with the killer whale, and the whale was more than happy to play with him, but the end result was a tragedy. There are some things that you cannot play with because they are not playing with you.

This is a sad story, because Daniel was the only child of his family back in South Carolina. Daniel was not a high school student. He was a twenty-six-year-old man who should have made better choices. Again we are reminded how important it is to think things through and make good choices. *Always remember the choices you make don't just affect you, but they also affect the people who love you.*

There are many things that you will be tempted to experiment with at some point in the future, but you need to remember this story. You need to realize that some things are not worth playing with.

Alcohol and drugs are not playing with you. Maybe you think it would be fun to have some beers at a weekend party with friends. You don't intend to be an alcoholic. You don't intend to have a problem. You don't intend to get addicted. You just want to try some weed. Maybe you think smoking a cigarette will make you appear more mature. Maybe you think people will take you more seriously if you do some of the things that older kids do. You've got to realize that while you think you are just playing around with alcohol, drugs, or tobacco, these things are deadly serious. They are not playing around with you. Alcohol and tobacco companies market their products to young people. They want to give you the impression that if you smoke and drink, you will have more fun, you'll be "cooler," and you'll be more attractive. These companies also know that the sooner you start using their products, the more money they can make. While you think you are just playing around with their products, they are deadly serious about getting you addicted. All you are to these people is a checkbook to squeeze as much money out of as they can.

There are a lot of things that are not playing with you. Maybe you're wondering about premarital sex. What's the big deal? You just want to check it out. You better think twice about that, because if you live for the moment, the moment will pass and you will regret it. Maybe you think it would be a great idea to send a picture of yourself to your boyfriend or girlfriend. You know the kind of picture I am talking about. You had better think that through. Once it's out there, you can't get it back.

Another thing not to be played with is an automobile. Cars are serious business. When you get behind the wheel of a car, you better fasten your seatbelt. You need to avoid distracted driving and pay attention to what is going on. Don't worry about what's on the radio or if someone is sending a text. Those things are not unimportant, but safe driving is extremely important. Lives depend on it.

Another thing that is not playing with you is the law. Maybe you are at the store and somebody dares you to take something that doesn't belong to you. You have the money to buy it if you want to, but you just want to see if you can take it without them noticing. Some might think that is exciting. I hope you don't, because it is not exciting—it's just stupid. "But I was just playing around. It was a joke. It's no big deal." It might not be a big deal to you, but it's a big deal to the owner of the store, and it's a big deal to the police who enforce the laws.

Daniel Dukes made a choice that turned out to be fatal. He did not intend for his life to end on July 5, 1999. He was playing around.

> We know that there are many things that you can't play around with because they have no intention of playing around with you.

45

DISCUSSION QUESTIONS

1. Why do we often think we can mess around with dangerous things?

2. Why do we always think "that couldn't happen to me"?

3. What are some things others claim are not dangerous but we should still avoid?

BIBLE PASSAGE FOR ADDITIONAL STUDY

11 Samuel 11:1–17

LIFE LESSON 8

THE CHOICES YOU MAKE AFFECT OTHERS

"No man is an island."
—John Donne

"Do you know that a little bit of leaven
leavens the whole lump?"
—I Corinthians 5:6

We talked in the last chapter a little bit about making choices. This expands on that theme. Some decisions that we make are much more important than what we wore to school or what we had for lunch.

Let me tell you a story to try to illustrate this point. Let's say you want to go to the basketball game on Friday night. It's a really big game. Everyone is going and you don't want to miss it. You ask your mom if you can go to the game. She says you can go, but you have to find your own ride home after the game. Your dad has a big presentation in Atlanta

Saturday morning, and your parents will have to get up at oh-dark-hundred. They will go to bed at nine p.m. because they have to get up so early to get to Atlanta and set up for the presentation. Your mom makes it clear that they cannot pick you up after the game. You understand completely and start looking for a ride home on Friday.

After searching high and low, you finally find someone who can take you home. He lives three doors down from you, and he is a responsible junior at your school. His name is Trent. He was working on his lawn and you asked him if he was going to the game. He said he was and that he would be glad to give you a ride home after the game. Trent says to meet him after the game by the fountain in the gym lobby. This is perfect. You can't wait for Friday night to come!

The game is very exciting, with several lead changes in the fourth quarter. The good guys win on a late three-point shot. The crowd storms the court after the victory over your bitter rival. You are excited and head out to the lobby to meet Trent. But Trent is not there. Come to think of it, you haven't seen Trent at the game all evening. You ask around. Finally, someone tells you that Trent got sick at school and went home. He is not at the game. You can't find anyone to take you home. Finally, a senior guy who you have seen around offers you a ride home. You barely know him. He's not a friend or even an acquaintance. People call him Snake and he calls his buddy Wild Thing. They're very loud, and it is obvious that they have had a couple of adult beverages. What would you do? Your mom made it clear that you could go to the game only if you found a ride home. You weren't planning on Trent getting sick. Would you ride with Snake?

> **You get to make choices, but you don't
> get to choose the consequences.**

What possible consequences could occur if you get in the car with these shady characters? Here are some possible consequences to this decision:

1) You might get home safely. You might. It's possible. But would you really want to risk your life, your health, and your reputation on *the chance* that you could get home? Not me.

2) You might get pressured to drink with them. Could you stand up to that pressure? Would you cave in? "Come on, man, just try it. You think you're better than us? Who are you, Susie Sunday school? Come on, Reverend. Give it a shot!"

3) You could go to jail. If Snake is driving erratically, the police would pull the car over. If there is an open container in the car, everybody goes to jail. Period! It doesn't matter if you haven't had anything to drink. An open container of alcohol in the car means everybody goes to jail. If you think Mom is going to be upset when you call her to come pick you up, imagine how angry she would be if you ask her to pick you up at the county jail rather than at the gym.

4) You could be in a wreck. Alcohol seriously impairs a person's ability to drive a car. They can hit a tree and you could be seriously hurt, crippled, or even killed. Breaking your arm could prevent you from a lot of activities that you enjoy. Being crippled and in a wheelchair is not even something we like to talk about, but it could happen.

5) You could be assaulted. These two shady characters

could take you way out of town. They could rob you. They could beat you up. Or worse!

What are we saying? You get to make choices, but you don't get to choose the consequences. If I go down to the convenience store and rob the clerk, the chances are that I will get caught. No doubt they have cameras for surveillance at the store, or a customer will take my video on their phone as I drive away. When I am caught, I confess. I cry. I feel bad. I had great intentions to give the money to my brother, who is a missionary in South America. I wanted to help him with his radio station. The fact of the matter is it doesn't make any difference how much I apologize or how badly I feel about what I have done. It doesn't matter that I wanted the money to go for a good cause. I made a bad choice, and now I don't get to choose the consequences. Whatever the judge decides is what will happen.

You get to make choices; you don't get to choose the consequences. I'm going to attempt to illustrate this life lesson in such a way that, hopefully, you will not forget it. This is a story—an illustration. *It never happened.* With God's help nothing like this will ever happen. This is just a story. I want to make this perfectly clear. Don't tell your parents, "Guess what Coach T. did." I am hopelessly in love with my wife. She is tremendous. I worshiped her from afar for almost two years before I got up the nerve to ask her out. I would never do anything to hurt her. But for the sake of illustration, here is the story.

Let's say I drive down to the Burger King to get lunch. The drive-through line is long, but there are no customers inside the store. I park my car and go in the store. The young girl at the counter is ready to take my order. But first she says, "Wow, you look good! Have you been working out?" I can't figure out who she's talking to. Since I am the only one in the store, I guess she's talking to me. So I say, "Yeah, I have been working out." (Technically, this is not a lie. I have a strenuous exercise program that I do every morning. One, two, three, four, and then I open and close my other eye four times. So yeah, I work out.) Then she says, "You really smell nice. What is that cologne that you are wearing?" I think about it. It's a little embarrassing, because I'm wearing Degree antiperspirant. So I say, "I'm wearing Calvin Hilfiger cologne for extremely masculine men." She says, "Of course you are." She takes my order. I pay for my meal. She writes her phone number on the back of my receipt. She says, "I get off at three. Call me and we can get better acquainted." Boy, am I confused!

Now, let's be clear on this. This is just a story—it's an illustration. It never happened. But let's say for the sake of illustration that I finished my lunch and finished the day teaching. Then I found the receipt and, in a moment of selfishness, weakness, stupidity, and insanity, I decided to call the number. She's excited to hear from me and says, "Pick me up at three." I proceed to Burger King and pick her up. We go to a nearby motel and have an affair. Thirty-five years of marriage faithfulness go down the drain. Reason was held hostage by insanity, and I make a decision that I will regret for the rest of my life. What might the consequences be from this infidelity?

Here's a list of some of the possible consequences that could result from this selfish act:

First, my wife might never find out. I suppose that is the best outcome that I could hope for. But how is this still harmful to me? Well, I would still have to live with the guilt of knowing what I had done. I would live in fear of being discovered. Every time the phone rang, every time the doorbell rang, and every time there was a knock on my classroom door I would be fearful. Is it the Burger Queen? Is she going to tell all? Will my wife, my children, and my students all learn that I am a phony? In many ways I think the guilt and fear would be even harder to live with than telling the truth.

It's possible my wife could find out and forgive me. My wife is a great person. She is truly amazing. Even if she did forgive me, and I can't be sure that she would, our marriage would still be irreparably harmed. A strong marriage is based on trust. Would our marriage ever be as strong as it was before the affair? Could she ever trust me again? I really doubt it. No matter how hard she might try, there would have to be lingering doubts about whether she could ever fully trust me again.

Third, she can become angry and hit me with the skillet. Who could blame her? I stood before God, family, and friends and promised to be faithful to her for as long as we both shall live. She has a right to expect me to keep my promise.

A fourth possible consequence is she could throw me out of our house and file for divorce. Wow, this is very hard to even think about. Remember: *we get to make choices, but we don't get to choose the consequences.*

Next, I could lose my family. I guarantee you the first call my wife would make if she found out I had been unfaithful to her would be to our daughter. Our daughter, Rachael, would call both of her brothers and tell them what I had done. They would all be bitter and angry toward me. Rightfully so! I made promises to them that I would always be there for them and their mother. They would lose all respect for me because my word was worthless. If I ever hurt their mother, they would be through with me from then on. I would not be welcome at dance recitals, Little League games, birthdays, or holidays. That is a lot to give up for a selfish act.

While that paints a pretty bleak picture, that is not even half of it. I have lost my wife, my kids, my grandchildren, my house, and my self-respect. And we are just getting warmed up! What if the Burger Queen calls and says I need to see a doctor and get tested for a sexually transmitted disease? Hey, when you decide to have sex with someone, not only are you having sex with them, but you are having sex with everyone they have ever had sex with. *Ugh!* Who knows how many guys the Burger Queen has been with? There are so many sexually transmitted diseases that it is mind-boggling. Some, like herpes, are viruses. You can never get rid of a virus. Herpes has been referred to as the gift that keeps on giving, because you will have it for the rest of your life. And of course, the HIV virus can lead to AIDS which can take your life.

What if the Burger Queen calls and claims that she is pregnant? Could she be pregnant? Could that child be mine? If she is pregnant and the child is mine, I will be responsible to pay child support for the next eighteen years. This would cost me tens of thousands of dollars, and I would have no way of knowing how she spent that money. She could spend the money for a new car or a cruise with her boyfriend, and I would have no say in the matter.

The Burger Queen could also demand hush money to keep our affair quiet. If I paid her, let's say, $10,000, would she go away? Would that be the end of it? Of course not! She would come back until I had no money left. She could also threaten to go to the police and tell them that I assaulted her. She could show pictures of bruises on her body and claim that I hurt her. (She actually is responsible for the bruises herself, but she has my DNA and it is her word against mine.) Do I want to risk my life on who the jury might believe? If I refuse to pay her, there is a very good chance the police will arrest me and charge me with a crime.

I would love to see one of my students on the front page of the newspaper. It would be great if the headline screamed: "TEENAGER SAVES BABY FROM BURNING BUILDING." I would be so proud. I would brag to all my friends. It would be so exciting. The governor might call you to the capitol to get an award. That would be great. Or it would be great if you hit a home run to win the regional championship for our baseball team and your picture was on the front page of the sports page. That would be exciting. But not all newspaper articles are equally exciting. I would not want to see my mug shot in the paper with the headline blaring, "COACH ARRESTED FOR SEXUAL ASSAULT." That would be really bad. Do you think I would be in a classroom today if that was in the paper? No way. Our principal would not let an accused felon in any classroom. Rightfully so! That would be so embarrassing—being asked to gather up my stuff and leave while my students watched me walk away in shame.

What I'm trying to say is that we get to make choices, but we don't get to choose the consequences. Look at all I would have lost: my wife, my kids, my grandchildren, my house, thousands of dollars, possibly my health, my freedom, and my job. Hey, I'm the guy down by the interstate with a cardboard sign that says "WILL COACH FOR FOOD." This is depressing just thinking about it. I have spent the last thirty-five years trying to build a reputation of character and stability. I would be a guy with no future . . . because of one bad choice.

Look at who would be hurt by my selfish choice. My wife would be hurt. Our sons and daughter would be hurt. Our grandchildren would be hurt. All of my former students would discard all I ever taught them. They would think, *What a hypocrite!* My former players would think the same thing. Young coaches I have tried to mentor would be confused. My church family would be stained by my mess. My parents, who have always set a good example for me, would be heartbroken because I would have dishonored our family's name. I have never been ashamed to be called a Templeton, because my parents have always maintained a great testimony for the Lord.

> **Be careful to think things through and make good choices.** *You get to make choices, but you don't get to choose the consequences.* **And never forget: your bad choices can hurt many other people.**

DISCUSSION QUESTIONS

1. Has anyone made a bad decision that adversely affected you?

2. If you broke the law, how would it affect others?

3. What are some bad decisions you could make, and how would they affect the important people in your life?

4. If you made one of those bad decisions, how would it change you?

BIBLE PASSAGE FOR ADDITIONAL STUDY

Joshua 7:10–26

HOW TO MAKE THE TOUGH CHOICES

"Some choices we live not only once
but a thousand times over,
remembering them for the rest of our lives."
—Richard Bach

"See, I have set before thee this day life and good,
and death and evil."
—Deuteronomy 30:15

We have talked a lot about the importance of decision-making. You understand that you get to make choices but you do not get to choose the consequences. You understand that if you live for the moment, the moment will pass and you will regret it. You understand that your choices will affect others.

- How can I make good decisions?
- How can I avoid silly mistakes?

- How can I say no when I am pressured to do something that I know is not right, moral, or safe?
- How can I find the strength to say no when pressured by the crowd?
- How can I say no to temptation when, on a date, there is a conflict between what my body says to do and what my mind knows is right?

If you wait to see what everyone else is doing to make a decision, too often you will give in to peer pressure. Even when you know better, even when you've been taught by your parents, it will be hard to say no to the crowd. Why is that? We all want to be accepted. We don't want to feel like we are missing out on something. We don't want other people to think that we are weird or "holier than thou." We don't want to be made fun of or ridiculed.

There are some times that you just need to take a stand. It doesn't matter what other people think. You need to do what you know is right. The easiest way to stand up and do the right thing at the moment of truth is to *decide ahead of time* that there are some things that you are not going to do. Period!

- It doesn't matter if the crowd laughs and makes fun of you.
- It doesn't matter if they say you are weird.
- It doesn't matter if they get offended.

> **Make the decision *now*. Make it *today*. *Right now!***
> **In your heart and mind, decide that there are**
> **some things that you are just not going to do.**

When you decide ahead of time that you are not going to use tobacco, you have made a good choice. Tobacco is not going to add any value to your life. It is a costly, nasty, and dangerous habit. It does not make you look more mature or make people take you more seriously. Decide today that tobacco will never be part of your life. I was once told by an acquaintance who had been addicted to alcohol and cocaine that tobacco is more addictive than anything he had ever done. He went to rehab and kicked alcohol. He doesn't use drugs, but he still smokes today.

The same can be said for alcohol, illegal drugs, premarital sex, cheating in school, wearing your seatbelt, driving responsibly, being honest, and so on. When you make decisions ahead of time, it simplifies things. Situations that could get complicated are much easier to deal with when you've already made the decision before the situation even arises.

For example, if you've already decided to drive carefully every time you get behind the wheel of a car, you will not be tempted when somebody asks you if you want to race. You've already decided that you're not going to do anything stupid while driving. If your phone goes off and you are receiving a text message while you are driving, you will probably be tempted to answer that text. This is not only dangerous, it is against the law. But it is a real temptation. However, since you have decided ahead of time to be a careful driver, the decision is already made, and the text will have to wait.

You could be tempted to cheat on a test. You got home late from the ballgame the night before. You meant to study, but you didn't have time. It could be very easy for you to give in to the temptation of cheating. You can justify it in your mind: it's not that big a deal, everybody does it, you won't get caught, no one will know, you need to keep your grades up, and your parents will be really mad if you fail a test. It would be easy to give in to temptation and fail this test of character. But you have already decided ahead of time that you don't want to be a cheater. You have decided that your character is more important than your GPA. Since you've already made this decision, the temptation is lessened considerably, and your character remains intact.

Let's say a couple is in the car on a date. The car is parked. The windows are fogged up. They are reading the Bible in the car. That's what they'd be doing, right? If one of them has made a decision ahead of time that there are some things that they are not going to do on a date, it will be a much easier decision. If you wait to make that decision in the heat of the moment, it will be much more difficult to do the right thing, even when you know what you should do in that situation.

I have already decided that I never want to take something that doesn't belong to me. It doesn't matter what it is. It doesn't matter if no one else will ever know. I will know. Sometimes we can be tempted to take something because we need it or we convince ourselves that we deserve it. This is called stealing. I don't want to be a thief. I want to protect my reputation at all times. I have found that this decision I made a long time ago has helped me many times when I could have been tempted.

In Genesis 39 we are given a great story that teaches us this valuable lesson. Joseph had been sold as a slave by his brothers to the Midianites. He was then resold to Potiphar in Egypt. Potiphar was an extremely successful man. He was a cabinet member. He probably traveled a lot on official business for the Pharaoh. The Bible doesn't specifically say, but we can guess that Potiphar was very wealthy. (We do know that he was greatly blessed because of Joseph.)

The Bible account tells us Potiphar's trophy wife wanted to have an affair with Joseph. Joseph was a handsome guy. He was probably about nineteen years old. He was away from his family. It would have been easy for Joseph to think the following:

- It's about time I caught a break. I deserve this.
- My family wouldn't approve—but they'll never know.
- No one will ever know.
- It's no big deal. We're consenting adults.
- Everybody does it.

> **Be careful about the lies you tell yourself.**

The question is, how could a teenager, full of testosterone, resist this tempting woman? A woman who relentlessly pursued him day after day? I think he realized all sin is against God. Second, he must have decided ahead of time that he was going to guard his character. *Deciding ahead of time draws the line and takes the emotion out of the decision-making process.*

Life can be very complicated. Sometimes you'll have to make some difficult decisions on the fly. It can be tricky. But many decisions can be greatly simplified if you just decide ahead of time that there are some things that you are not going to do.

> **Decide ahead of time that there are some things that you are not going to do. Period!**

DISCUSSION QUESTIONS

1. How can deciding ahead of time help you avoid cheating or stealing?

2. How can decisions you make ahead of time affect your dating life?

3. How can you find the strength to say no when pressured by the crowd?

4. If Joseph was nineteen when he was tempted in Egypt, how could he say no to temptation?

5. What types of temptation—choices—should you take off the table and never consider?

BIBLE PASSAGES FOR ADDITIONAL STUDY

Genesis 39:9

Daniel 1:8

THE CRUCIAL CHOICE

"Has this world been so kind to you
that you should leave with regret?
There are better things ahead than any
we leave behind."
—C. S. Lewis

"I am the Way, the Truth, and the Life.
No man cometh unto the Father, but by me."
—John 14:6

I will make a lot of decisions today.
- Where will I eat?
- What will I have to eat?
- What will I wear?
- Will I go get my driver's license renewed today?
- Should I trade in my car for that new truck I saw advertised in the newspaper? I really want it . . . but do I need it?

Not all decisions are created equal. Some are much more important than others. I might get heartburn if I eat too much spicy food, but the discomfort would only last for a while. The clothes I wear today probably won't matter much either.

Then there are bigger decisions.

- How hard will you work in school?
- Will you graduate? Will you go to college?
- Where will you attend college?
- Will you date?
- What type of person will you date?
- What will you do/not do on a date?
- Who will you marry?
- How seriously will you take your marriage vows?
- Will you have kids?
- How many kids will you have?
- How strict will you be as a parent with your kids?
- What job will you have?
- Will you go to church?
- What type of church will you go to?
- How often will you attend?

Wow! These are some pretty serious questions. These are much more important than whether I go to the game tonight or stay home and read a book. But there is one question that is so important that it trumps all the others:

Where will I spend eternity?

We all have a problem in that we are sinners. Sin is falling short of the standard that God requires from us. The best person you know sins. We tend to rank sins according to severity. For example, telling a white lie is a small sin, while abusing a small child would be unspeakably wicked. God doesn't look at it like that. He is holy and He cannot stand sin.

On the other side of the coin, God is love. He loves all sinners. He loves everyone. No one is excluded from God's love. He cares about every single person. He loves Buddhists, Muslims, Jews, Christians, atheists, agnostics, whatever. Your label (Catholic, Baptist, Church of God, Methodist, etc.) is not important; *your relationship to God is paramount.*

God had a dilemma. He loves sinners, but He hates sin. He is holy. He can't just overlook our sin. His holiness demands that sin must be paid for. If God punished us for our sins, it would frustrate His love. How could God satisfy His love and His holiness?

John 3:16 and 17 tell us how God was able to satisfy both His love and His holy nature. He gave his son to die so that we might accept his gift of eternal life. Jesus, the sinless son of God, died on the cross to pay the debt for your sins and mine. This satisfies a holy God's demand for justice. At the same time it allows a loving God to satisfy his love by offering us the gift of everlasting life.

Some people have the wrong idea about God. They think He is a cosmic killjoy who is mad at us because of our sins or hates us because of our disobedience. This is not true. He loves us and wants the best for us. He hates our sins and is grieved when we sin.

I'm going to try to illustrate this by tweaking a story from Max Lucado's great book, *Just Like Jesus*.

My wife, Vicky, watches our two youngest grandsons usually once a week. Our daughter Rachael is an NICU nurse like her mom. They sometimes work together in the same pod at the hospital. Usually, one day a week the boys stay at Nana's house. Jake is three years old. Luke is one year old. Jake especially loves the playroom at Nana's house. It has puppets, cars, books, puzzles, farm animals, dinosaurs, etc. He especially loves it when Nana gets down on the floor to play with him.

He also loves to go outside. Let's say Nana takes Jake outdoors while Luke stays inside and takes a nap with Big Daddy. That's what my grandkids call me. Jake runs, slides, swings, climbs, and plays. And falls a lot! It's a good thing Nana is there to cure all the scrapes with a kiss.

Let's suppose Jake is playing in the sandbox with a pail and a shovel. Nana hears the ice cream truck coming down the street. While keeping an eye on Jacob, she slips over and buys him an ice cream sandwich. She brings it back and he smiles at her. His mouth is full of sand and dirt.

Does Nana leave him with sand in his mouth? Of course not! She would rinse his mouth out. He might strenuously object. He likes to be in the gritty sandbox. But Nana loves him, just like he is, cleans him up, and gives him a treat.

> **"God loves you just as you are, but he refuses to leave you that way." —Max Lucado**

67

It doesn't matter what you've done. You are never too far gone to turn from your sin and to Him. The emptiness you have in your heart cannot be filled by material things, pleasure, fame, recognition, or status. The hole in our souls can only be filled by a relationship with God.

Have you made the *crucial choice* to put your never-dying soul in His hands? It's the best choice I ever made.

DISCUSSION QUESTIONS

1. What are some things that may prevent you from making the crucial choice?

2. Why do we call this the crucial choice?

3. Have you ever heard anybody say they regretted accepting Christ as Savior?

4. What are some things people use to try to fill the void that only Christ can fill?

BIBLE PASSAGES FOR ADDITIONAL STUDY

John 14:6

John 3:16

THERE ARE TWO WAYS TO LEARN

"Most people don't listen with the intent to understand:
they listen with the intent to reply."
—Stephen Covey

"My son, attend to my words;
incline thine ear to my sayings.
Let them not depart from thine eyes . . ."
—Proverbs 4:21, 22

The choice is yours. Whether you believe it or not, many people want to help you. Your parents, your grandparents, your teachers, your youth pastor, and your Uncle Roy all want to see you do well. They all want you to be happy. They have learned some things the hard way. Your parents don't want to keep you from anything that is fun or profitable or beneficial for you. They want the best for you. Many times young people think that their parents are old and don't have any fun, so they don't want them to have any fun.

Your parents have made mistakes in the past, and sometimes they have the scars to prove it. So listen to them, trust their experience. They know what they are talking about.

Our grandson Jacob comes over often to stay at our house. Sometimes Nana tells Jacob to be careful not to touch the burner in the kitchen. She tells him the burner is very hot. She tells him he can get hurt if he touches the stove. At this point, Jacob has a decision to make. He can trust Nana and listen to her advice or he can ignore Nana. He can think that Nana is trying to keep him from having fun. I mean, after all, the burner on the stove is a pretty orange color, and it looks like it would be very amusing to play with. He can convince himself that he knows better than Nana. After all, he is three years old. The choice is his: he can listen to Nana or he can burn his hand. He gets to decide. If he decides incorrectly he will get burned. Nana doesn't get to choose for him. It is his decision, and he has to live with the choice he makes.

When your parents or teachers give you advice about temptations that face you in your life, they are speaking from experience. They faced some of those same temptations. Sometimes, they made the wrong decisions and they paid the price for those poor decisions. If you listen to them, you can learn from their mistakes. They might be talking to you about alcohol or tobacco and the dangers associated with these things. They have seen how using tobacco over a period of years can adversely affect your health. They have seen alcohol enslave and destroy some of their friends and family members. They are fully aware of the consequences of using these products. They know the beer commercials on TV don't tell the whole story. They don't want you to get burned. Will you listen to them? The choice is yours. If you listen to your parents and teachers, you can avoid the pain, embarrassment, and regret that accompany a bad decision.

I like to play golf. Sometimes we will be enjoying a round of golf and someone in another group will yell "Fore!" with a sense of urgency. "Fore" means "Hey, look out. I just skulled a shot horribly and it is coming toward you." They want you to take cover, and quickly! What do you think I do when a golfer yells "Fore!"? Do you think I holler "Seven!" or some other number at them to be funny? Do you think I tell them to be quiet because I'm concentrating on my next shot? Do you think I just ignore them?

The correct answer is none of the above. I have seen people get hit by a golf ball. Getting hit by a golf ball would hurt like crazy. You could be seriously hurt by someone's misdirected missile. If I hear someone yell "Fore!" I don't ignore it. I duck behind a tree, or a golf cart, or my son-in-law. (Sorry, V.)

I can learn by listening or by a lump on the head. The same goes for you. You choose whether to listen to warnings or not. *Choose wisely, because there are consequences to your decisions.*

The guy with *little ears* is sad because he didn't listen!

DISCUSSION QUESTIONS

1. What was the best advice someone ever gave you?

2. What are some of the types of people you should listen to?

3. Who are the types of people you should ignore?

4. Do you have someone in your life who will tell you the truth and not just what you want to hear?

BIBLE PASSAGES FOR ADDITIONAL STUDY

Proverbs 2:1–5

Psalm 119:18

THE MOST IMPORTANT FUNDAMENTAL

"I have no choice about whether or not
I have Parkinson's;
I have nothing but choices about how
I react to it."
—Michael J. Fox

"Let this mind be in you, which was
also in Christ Jesus."
—Philippians 2:5

I coached college basketball for eight seasons. We had a lot of fun. If there's one thing I learned from coaching college basketball it is that you had better recruit some very good players. If you have good players, you will be a good coach. If you have average players, you will be an average coach. If you have championship players, you will have a championship-caliber team. And if you have really bad players, you will be selling insurance very soon. Recruiting is the key to having a good team in college basketball. You look for good players that can help you reach your goals.

What do you think is the most important thing that a college basketball coach looks for in a prospective student-athlete?

Some would say that you look for guys that can shoot the ball. Shooting is very important, but it's not the most important thing that you look for. It has been said that offense sells tickets, but defense wins games. Playing good defense is crucial in college basketball, but it is not the most important thing. College basketball is a very tough sport, played by very tough people. It is very difficult to hang a banner unless your players rebound the ball extremely well. But toughness and rebounding ability are secondary to something else when it comes to recruiting prospective student-athletes.

The most important thing that a coach is looking for is a good attitude. It doesn't matter how talented a player is if he has a bad attitude. We stopped recruiting him if we became aware that his attitude was poor.

> **A good attitude can cover a multitude of sins.**
> **A bad attitude is often contagious**
> **and can sink the entire ship.**

We saw a player at the state tournament that was truly amazing. He was six feet seven inches tall and could run like a deer. He could shoot from long range and could pass and dribble the ball like a point guard. This guy could jump over the moon. He could play almost any position on the court. This is very important at a small school where you have a limited number of scholarships. Recruiting a player who could play two or three different positions was almost like having an extra scholarship. It was huge. We were so excited about this player.

After the game, I talked to the player's coach. I introduced myself and congratulated him on their excellent showing at the state tournament. He thanked me, and I told him we were interested in one of his players who was graduating that year, number 45. He laughed and said he doubted that number 45 would be graduating. He would be using up his eligibility, but it was doubtful he would have enough credits to graduate.

I asked him if number 45 had a good attitude and he said no. "He is a pain in the neck. He is selfish and un-coachable. He criticizes his teammates and all he cares about are his own personal stats. If he scores thirty points and we lose, he is happy. If he scores eight or ten points and we win, he is angry and pouts. He is a pain in the #$%."

I thanked him for his time and wished him well in the rest of the playoffs. Do you think I asked this player to visit our campus? Do you think we went to his home for a recruiting visit with his parents? No way! A college basketball season is six months long. You have to love the players you coach, or you will be miserable. Recruiting a new player is much like adopting someone into your family. If the pieces don't fit together, everyone is miserable. We didn't waste one more second recruiting that talented head case. It doesn't matter how well you can shoot the ball or play defense if your attitude stinks.

> "Our attitudes are either the fuel that propels us to victory, or the mud that bogs us down in defeat." —Shad Helmstetter

Is your attitude the fuel that moves you to victory? Or are you bogged down, spinning your tires but getting nowhere because of your attitude? If you are working hard but can't seem to get anywhere, it could be that your attitude is holding you back. You are like a hamster running on a wheel: a lotta effort, no results.

At the end of her life, Helen Keller wrote, "I have found life to be so beautiful." How could she say that? Helen Keller was blind, deaf, and mute. I cannot imagine how difficult it would be to be blind. My wife and I went out to Arizona on spring break a couple of years ago. We had a wonderful trip. We saw amazing sites like the Grand Canyon and the red rocks at Sedona, Arizona. There are no pictures that do the Grand Canyon justice. There are no words to adequately describe the beauty and grandeur of this remarkable place. But Helen Keller never saw the Grand Canyon.

Have you ever seen a toddler learning to walk? Or a two-year-old eating a cupcake? Have you seen a puppy get excited and come running to greet you when you got home from a trip? He is excited and wagging his tail. These are also some of the simple pleasures of life that Helen Keller never saw.

Last week our little granddaughter hugged me at her birthday party. She turned six years old. She smiled and kissed me and said, "I love you, Big Daddy." Helen Keller never heard a little child tell her that she was loved or saw the joy of a six-year-old at her birthday party.

How could Helen Keller say that she had found life to be so beautiful? Maybe a better question would be, why do we complain so much? You see, Helen Keller understood that you don't just live in your body, but you live in your mind. Helen Keller decided that life would be beautiful, and it was. She graduated from college and she raised millions of dollars for foundations that still help thousands of people today.

In contrast to Helen Keller, let's take a look at Napoleon Bonaparte. He said, "I have never known six happy days in my life." Napoleon was the emperor of France. He controlled almost all of Western Europe. He had everything that this life could offer someone. He had fame, power, respect, material things, riches, you name it.

He had the best clothes, and all were tailor-made. He had the most beautiful horses and a BMW chariot. If he wanted something to eat, he just clapped his hands. Servants would immediately run and retrieve him some French toast or some French fries or a six-pack of Coke. Whatever he wanted, he could have. He lived in a palace.

Yet at the end of his life, Napoleon claimed he had never known six happy days in his entire life. That's a very revealing statement, and a sad one. Hey, I had seven happy days just last week! How could he be so miserable? Another statement that Napoleon made may shed some light on his outlook. He said, "I only like men who are useful to me, and only for as long as they are useful." I think Napoleon was miserable because he was self-absorbed. His focus was on himself and what he wanted. He saw other people as disposable items to be used and then thrown away like a box of tissues. When you see people in this light, you will be miserable. Helen Keller had a great attitude because her focus was on others, not on herself. Helen Keller saw life as a beautiful venture to be enjoyed, not as a marathon race to be endured.

I cannot emphasize enough the importance of a good attitude for your future success. It will be virtually impossible to have a successful marriage if you struggle with your attitude. It will be hard to get a job, keep a job, get a promotion, take care of your family, or even have a happy home if a member of the family has attitude problems. No business, church, neighborhood, or ball team can be successful if individuals have poor attitudes.

A recent Harvard study found that success is 15 percent ability and 85 percent attitude. There are a lot of unsuccessful people who have a lot of ability, but their attitude keeps them from achieving even half of what they could if they had their head on straight.

> **Allow your attitude to take you to
> the next level in your life.**

DISCUSSION QUESTIONS

1. How could Helen Keller have such a good attitude?

2. Why do you think Napoleon had such a bad attitude?

3. What can you do on a personal level to improve your attitude?

4. Why is happiness so elusive?

BIBLE PASSAGE FOR ADDITIONAL STUDY

Philippians 2:5–11

THE ONLY ONE WHO CAN CHOOSE

"You can bear your troubles or shrug them off.
They're your shoulders."

—Robert Brault

"And Elijah came unto all the people, and said,
how long halt ye between two opinions?"

—I Kings 18:21

Who is responsible for the attitude you have right now? If your coach yelled at you at practice yesterday, did he give you a bad attitude? If your boss is under an immense amount of pressure and yelled at you this morning, is your attitude his fault? If you are late to school and get a tardy because of your sister, and that results in you getting a detention, is your angry attitude her fault? If somebody swerved into your lane, endangering your life, is your anger justified?

Nope. *You are responsible for your attitude. I am responsible for my attitude. Only you can decide what your attitude will be. No one else can decide that for you.* It doesn't matter what other people do or say. It doesn't matter what the weather is like outside or how much money I have in my bank account. These things do not determine my attitude. I determine my attitude.

I'm sure there are many times when my wife wishes she could go to Walmart and pick up an attitude-adjusting remote control. Boy, wouldn't that be great if I could invent a remote control that would allow me to dial up a good attitude for other people? I could probably sell millions and millions of those for $200 apiece. I imagine my wife would probably be the first in line to buy one of those! She'd probably buy a couple so she'd have a backup. Unfortunately, no such gizmo exists. You are the only one who can control your attitude, and I am the only person who can decide what my attitude will be.

John Milton was an English writer. He said, "The mind is its own place, and in itself can make a heaven of hell or a hell of heaven." He understood the same thing that Helen Keller had figured out: you don't just live in your body; you also live in your mind.

You decide whether you are going to like a class or not. Only you! I hope you'll enjoy all of your classes, but I don't get a vote. You will have to decide for yourself if this is going to be a good day or a bad one. The choice is yours. It is totally up to you. Your outlook, your frame of mind, is your attitude. No one can decide that for you.

When I got up this morning, I didn't flip a coin to see if it was going to be a good day or a bad day. I didn't see what the weather would be like before I decided what my attitude would be. I didn't check the balance in my bank account to see if I was going to have a good day or a bad day. I didn't look to see if my favorite blue shirt was clean so I could wear it today. I didn't wait to see how I felt. All of these things are circumstantial, and I don't want to be ruled by circumstance or by emotions. Weak people are ruled by their emotions or by how they feel. "Well, I just don't feel like going to work today" or "My diabetes is acting up today, so I'm in a bad mood" are just excuses.

Don't be ruled by your circumstances. Rise above them. Take responsibility for your attitude, and you will be much more productive as you work your way through the day. Never blame others for your bad attitude, because you are the only one who can decide what your attitude will be.

> Not only are you the only person who can decide what your attitude will be, but you have to decide what your attitude will be every day.

I have to choose every day what my attitude will be like. You choose every day what your attitude will be like. If you chose to have a great attitude yesterday, good choice! Congratulations! That was a good move on your part. I bet you had a great day yesterday because you chose a winning attitude. But today is a new day, and you'll have to choose what your attitude will be again today. So will I.

Not only do we have to choose our attitude each and every day, we have to decide to have a great attitude many times throughout the day. Life is hard. It can be challenging. You can be disappointed many times throughout the day when things don't go as planned. So not only do we have to choose to have a winning attitude first thing in the morning, we have to choose to continue to have a winning attitude when things don't go our way.

When things go wrong, do you whine, gripe, and complain to others? Do you look for someone else to blame? Do you make excuses or do you adjust? Life gets messy, and when things get difficult, we have to choose what our attitude will be when things don't necessarily go as planned.

Our youngest son, Mitch, and I were driving to the store to get some snacks for our trip to Columbus, Ohio. We were excited because we were going the next day to see the Ohio State Buckeyes play football at the Horseshoe. He asked if he could drive my new car to the store. I said sure. We got our snacks and were headed back home.

Mitch stopped when the traffic light turned red, but the driver behind us did not see that the light changed. We heard tires skidding and then a crash as we were slammed from behind. We never saw it coming. I asked Mitch if he was all right. He was a little shaken, but he was uninjured. We got out of the car to see what had happened.

A young mother was in the car behind us. Her little girl was screaming. The driver was crying and visibly shaken but did not appear to be injured. What do you think was my next move at this point?

Do you think I…

- Cursed loudly at her, berating her for not paying closer attention?
- Threatened to sue her and made a sarcastic remark about women drivers?
- Or asked if she was all right?

Of course, I asked if she was all right. I told her to get her baby out of the car and be sure that she was okay. Her child was about one year old. She had lost her pacifier, which was pinned to her shirt. The baby became upset when she couldn't get her pacifier. The mother was trying to drive and reach back to help her daughter with the pacifier at the same time. She did not see the light change colors. When she turned around she saw that we had stopped. She slammed on her brakes, but it was too late.

Losing my temper was not going to make the situation any better. I understood her situation. Our daughter, Rachael, was about her age and she had two little ones in diapers at that time. (Sometimes considering what another person is going through can keep us from overreacting. I probably should remember that more often.)

The fact of the matter is I wish I could choose to have a winning attitude once and have that settle the attitude issue forever. It just doesn't work that way. It's a battle that must be fought and won every day and even several times throughout the day.

Captain Jack Sparrow may have summarized it for us when he said, "The problem is not the problem. The problem is your attitude about the problem."

Charles Swindoll, a pastor and author from Fullerton, California, wrote, "Life is 10 percent what happens to me and 90 percent how I react to what happens." If it's pouring down rain, if the referee blows the call, if you overslept thirty minutes, if your wife burns the meatloaf, none of those things are nearly as important as your reaction to those challenges. And you will choose your attitude several times throughout most days.

DISCUSSION QUESTIONS

1. Do you ever look to someone else to make you happy?

2. What would be some things that could prevent you from being happy?

3. What can you do today to pursue happiness in your own life?

4. What could you do to get your day off to a good start?

BIBLE PASSAGES FOR ADDITIONAL STUDY

Numbers 14:24

Ephesians 4:2

FIND YOUR SWEET SPOT

"Talent wins games,
but teamwork wins championships."
—Michael Jordan

"Alone we can do so little;
together we can do so much."
—Helen Keller

Charlie Plumb graduated from the US Naval Academy. He was a fighter pilot who helped start the "Top Gun" school in Miramar, California. He flew seventy-five missions in F-4 and F-14 Tomcat Phantom jets over Hanoi off the USS *Kitty Hawk*.

On his seventy-fifth mission, just five days before he was to rotate off active duty, Plumb's plane was hit by a surface-to-air missile. The plane was on fire and would not respond. The stick was frozen. Finally, Charlie and his radar man ejected from the F-4 and parachuted, to be captured by angry North Vietnamese soldiers. Captain Plumb spent almost six years in the Hanoi Hilton, a notoriously tough prison. There he faced torture, hunger, filth, and oppressive jungle heat. He went into prison at twenty-four years of age and was released at age thirty after a prisoner exchange.

Charlie was eating dinner in a Kansas City restaurant when a guy a couple of tables over was staring at him. The stranger got up and approached Charlie's table. He said, "You're Charlie Plumb. You flew seventy-four successful missions off the USS *Kitty Hawk*. On your seventy-fifth mission you were shot down over Hanoi and captured. You spent six years as a POW at the Hanoi Hilton. You got out when they had a prisoner exchange."

Charlie told the man he was right. But there were hundreds of men on that ship. An aircraft carrier is huge. It's like a floating city. He was sorry, but he didn't remember the stranger. 'Who are you?' he asked. 'I'm the man who packed your parachute,' the man answered. Charlie thanked him for doing his job well. He asked him if he knew how many parachutes he had packed. The man said, "No, I never counted. I was just glad I had the opportunity to serve." John Maxwell told that story in his book *The 17 Indisputable Laws of Teamwork*. Dr. Maxwell calls this the Law of the Niche. In other words, everybody has a place in which they add the most value to the team. Not everybody gets to be a fighter pilot. Not everybody gets to wear wings on their uniform and have people count their successful missions. Somebody has to be willing to pack the parachutes.

Think about it. What if the parachute packer was resentful of all the attention a fighter pilot received? The parachute packer, no doubt, wore the generic navy uniform. No fancy jumpsuit with wings on it. No helmet, just that goofy little white hat.

Nobody counted his successes. Nobody ever gave him an "Attaboy! Whoa, that's the best job of packing a parachute I've ever seen!" It would be easy to think that no one cared or no one noticed all the hard work he put in. If a pilot gets shot down and killed, nobody is gonna say, "I bet it was the parachute packer's fault. If he'd done a better job of packing that parachute the pilot would still be alive today."

It would be easy for the parachute packer to slack off or get careless. He could have a bad day. Or week! He could easily convince himself that his work really doesn't matter. *Nobody notices me. Nobody cares. They treat those pilots like rock stars. I get no respect. What difference does it make? I think I'll just take the afternoon off.*

He didn't do that. He did his job. I bet Charlie Plumb was really glad he did. Charlie's life depended on that parachute packer not having an "off" day.

This lesson has two applications for each of us. First, we all need to find the spot where we can add the most value to our team, class, business, church, or family. Some guys are great catchers but they can't play shortstop. Some offensive linemen are extremely good blockers and are adept at protecting the quarterback. They add great value to the team, but that doesn't mean we want them to run with the

Find your sweet spot.

football. At church some sing, some preach, some play an instrument, and some work in the nursery.

Second, there are people in your past who have worked hard to help you get to where you are today. It might be a parent, or a teacher, or a friend, or a coach. Take a minute to thank them for their help. Be sure they realize that you are fully aware of the extra effort they made on your behalf. Or the time they invested in you. Or the sacrifices they made to allow you to pursue your dreams. It wouldn't take long for you to text, to call, or to drop them a note to say thanks for their investment in your life. It would mean the world to them, and you'd be a better person for it.

DISCUSSION QUESTIONS

1. Have you ever had a job or role on a team where you felt like a square peg in a round hole?

2. Have you ever had a job that just fits you?

3. How can a leader show appreciation for each person's role on the team?

4. What is your role in your family, at church, or on your team?

BIBLE PASSAGES FOR ADDITIONAL STUDY

Romans 12:4

I Corinthians 12:12–27

DON'T JUMP
TO CONCLUSIONS

"If judging people on first impressions
were an Olympic sport,
they'd suspect me of using steroids."
—Zaid Abdelnour

"Judge not, that ye be not judged."
—Matthew 7:1

What if four adults intentionally inflicted pain on a little three-year-old girl? They conspired against her. She is traumatized. They intentionally ignore her fear and her cries. She is hurt. They know what they are doing. They know she is scared. It is no accident. She is a tiny, scared child. What should happen to those cruel adults? Would you put them in jail?

My wife and I had only been married a few weeks. It was late July 1979. I drove to play golf with a friend from college,

Marc Dalton. We went to the Chippewa Country Club in Toledo, Ohio, where Marc lived. The club had a twilight special that allowed golfers to play as many holes as you could get after 1:00 p.m. for a set price. I think it was $12. Since we didn't have much money, this was a great deal for us. We played until it was too dark to even see the ball. It was after 9:00 p.m. I would guess we played forty-five or fifty holes. We were practically sprinting around the course. We both played pretty well and had a blast.

When we finished playing it was dark. We agreed to play the next month at a course near my house. I stopped at the Kewpie and got a couple of burgers for the ride home. I was tired but had greatly enjoyed the day.

When I was about halfway home my old clunker started making a loud noise. I was about to pull over when oil covered the windshield and smoke started rolling out from under the hood. The car lost power. The engine was knocking loudly. I had thrown a rod through the engine. I coasted off to the side of the road on I-75, somewhere near Findlay, Ohio.

It was around 10:15 p.m. and was probably 80 degrees or so. I got out, trying to figure out my next move. (Remember, there weren't cell phones in 1979.) The oil on the hot engine created a ton of smoke. I needed to walk to the nearest exit. I needed to find a pay phone to call my wife. She would call a friend to come get me.

I was standing there trying to remember how far I had gone past the last exit. Would it be shorter to walk to the next exit up or to go back? While I pondered my predicament, a guy on a motorcycle passed me. I saw his brake lights come on as he pulled over in the emergency lane on the right. He turned around and drove toward my stalled but still smoking junker. He was a big guy on a big bike. Check that. He was huge (think Coke machine with a head). I thought about opening the trunk to get a golf club handy, in case he wanted to rob me. After I remembered that I only had two bucks in my pocket, I decided I would not do anything stupid. I would just give him the cash if robbery was what he had in mind.

Did I mention he was *enormous*? He had long, greasy hair that fell four to six inches below the top of his shoulders. He had a scruffy beard and sleeves of tattoos down both arms. He was just a biscuit or two under 350 pounds. I had no idea what would happen next.

He watched the smoke for a few seconds and said, "That looks like where she laid last." I laughed and told him he was right. He asked if it was knocking loudly before it stalled out. I said it was. He confirmed what I had guessed. A rod was thrown through the engine, causing it to seize up.

I asked which way was the nearest exit. He said, "Where ya headed?" He genuinely wanted to help me. I told him I lived in Lima. He said, "That's only a half an hour away. I'll run you home." I told him it was the third of four Lima exits: the 309 exit. We live right behind Memorial Hospital. "It's at least an hour from here, maybe more." I didn't want him to commit to more than what it really was. He said, "Hop on. I'll have you home in thirty minutes. And I'm Bruce. Who are you?"

Now, remember in Ohio you don't have to wear a helmet on a motorcycle. Ohioans love their freedom; they don't like the government telling them what they can and cannot do. If they think helmets are for wusses, they don't want to be told they have to wear a helmet on a motorcycle. They want the right to crack their skull on the asphalt if they so desire. (By the way, I have had two very good friends seriously hurt on motorcycles. I try to avoid motorcycles since I wrecked one while dating the girl who became my wife. It was her dad's. Ouch.)

Well, I had a choice to make. Walk to a gas station, which was who knows how far away, or get on that Harley with some dude named Bruce. He was a total random with long hair and tats. Hey, not many people in 1979 had a lip ring and a nose ring as large as my wedding band. It wasn't an easy choice.

I got on the bike. I held on to the seat behind me. (No way was I holding onto him, that's how rumors get started.) I had no helmet, but a lot of fear. We took off as if we were shot from a cannon. It was freezing on that Harley. I just had a golf shirt and shorts on. Bruce passed everything in sight. He swerved from lane to lane. We were flying low. I looked over his shoulder and saw we were going 105 mph. I only looked once. I was afraid to see after that, but I could tell by how fast things were going by that we were going F-A-S-T.

As we approached the 309 exit, I tapped Bruce on the shoulder. It was a relief to see that the Harley had a brake and that he knew where it was. Three turns from the exit and we were in my driveway.

Bruce shut it down and I got off. He pulled out a pocket watch and said, "Hey, only twenty-seven minutes. Told ya." (Technically he was right in his estimated time of arrival, but he had the advantage of knowing that we would be exceeding the speed of sound.) I asked if I could get him a Coke or a glass of water. He said a Coke sounded good, so we headed into the house.

While I was in the kitchen getting two sixteen-ounce bottles of Coke, my wife came out of our bedroom where she had been reading. I entered the living room and my wife and Bruce were just standing there looking at one another. I am sure she was wondering who this *huge* biker was standing in our living room. I introduced them and told Vicky that our car was done for and that Bruce had stopped to see if he could help. I was hoping for a ride to the nearest pay phone, but he brought me all the way home from the other side of Findlay. "Wow, that's over an hour from here," she said. I told her it wasn't that far, and when she started to disagree, I told her I'd explain later. Bruce had a little snicker on that one.

We drank the Coke and I went back to our room to get $20 to give to Bruce. I thanked him again. I told him I wanted to at least buy him a burger for helping me out. Bruce said, "Put your money away, friend. I didn't help you to get some money." I insisted, but he never even considered taking the cash. (My guess is he saw the tiny house we lived in and realized we didn't have mad stacks of Benjamins.)

He said he had to go, but could he ask me a couple of questions first. I said sure. He asked if I was one of those "church guys." I said, "You mean a Christian?" He said, "Yeah, that's what you call it, a Christian. Are you a Christian?" I said I was. I asked him why he thought that I was "one of those church guys." He said, "Well you got a real straight-arrow haircut. You offered me a Coke instead of a beer, and I saw a calendar from your church over on the wall."

Bruce then asked me if he was stranded on the highway with a smoking engine in his old truck would I stop to see if I could help him. It was a tough question. I told him without hesitating, "No, no, I would not stop to help." He asked, "Why not?" I said, "Because you are scary. You are probably six four and a very imposing guy. You have that long hair and those tats. You are a biker with that huge beard. Nope, I'm not stopping." I'm not proud of that, but I probably weighed a buck sixty back then. I just tried to stay out of other people's way, especially if they were XXXL bikers.

He laughed. He wasn't offended at all. He knew I had told him the truth. He said, "You're a young guy. I am not talking down to you, but let me help you. Coach, you can't judge a book by its cover. Not all bikers are outlaws lookin' to rob ya. Don't jump to conclusions. Get all the facts."

With that, Bruce said he needed to go. I thanked him again. We shook hands. He went out, fired up his chopper, and left.

So today's life lesson number fifteen comes from a biker.

> **You can't judge a book by its cover. Don't jump to conclusions. Get all the facts.**

I gotta be honest. The younger generation is better at this than mine. Young people as a whole tend to give others the benefit of the doubt better than the older generations. I realize this is a generalization, but it is the truth. As a general rule, most young people are a little more tolerant and accepting of others who are different from them. Watch children at a playground. They usually are quick to join in with the other kids, regardless of their appearance. They don't even notice.

Bruce, the biker, had it right. Don't try to judge a book by its cover. Don't jump to conclusions. Get all the facts. All people have value and they shouldn't be prejudged due to ignorant stereotypes. It shouldn't matter if they have tattoos, dreadlocks, a Mohawk, or a purple frohawk. Give 'em a chance.

By the way, remember the story about the little girl who was intentionally hurt by those four adults? That is a true story also. She is my granddaughter, Elena. The four adults are her mom, dad, a nurse, and her pediatrician. They had

to hold her down to give her shots so she wouldn't get certain diseases like polio. They had to hurt her to help her. (Parents have to do that sometimes.)

Did you jump to conclusions or get all the facts? Some of you were upset. You were ready to send those adults to prison. But you didn't have all the facts.

Let's learn this good lesson from Bruce the Biker.

Don't jump to conclusions. Give people a chance.

DISCUSSION QUESTIONS

1. Why are we quick to judge others?

2. Why do we expect the benefit of the doubt from others?

3. Tell us about a time when you misjudged someone and found out you were wrong.

4. Who were some people that the Pharisees misjudged but Jesus hung out with?

BIBLE PASSAGE FOR ADDITIONAL STUDY

Matthew 7:1–5

BECOME AN EXPERT AT FORGIVENESS

"Forgiveness is a virtue of the brave."
—Indira Gandhi

"As far as the east is from the west,
so far hath he removed our transgressions from us."
—Psalm 103:12

Has anyone ever wronged you in such a way that it would be impossible for you to forget? Are you angry today at someone? Maybe a friend or relative betrayed your trust. Maybe a friend took something from you. Maybe a teacher misunderstood and mistreated you.

Do you get angry all over again when you think about the pain that you felt? Have you ever spent a lot of time planning to get even or punish them for what they have done? Have you ever heard someone say, "I'll forgive you, but I won't forget"?

It is very hard to forgive. We understand life is not fair, but we still find it hard to accept when the circumstances go against us.

Bitterness only hurts you. The person you are harboring resentment against isn't hurt by your anger. The vast majority of the time they aren't even aware of your feelings. If they were aware of your resentment, they would probably even enjoy it. The person hurt most by your bitterness is you.

If you dam up your resentment, it will build up inside of you. Eventually, that anger will erupt and overflow in an outburst. Often you lash out at someone else, someone you care about and don't intend to hurt. Then you have hurt yourself by damaging a relationship that really matters to you.

It is really important to understand a couple of things forgiveness is not. First, it is not forgetting. Some things are devastatingly bad and can't be forgotten. You don't have to be able to completely erase what happened from your memory.

Second, there is a difference between trust and forgiveness. It is possible to forgive someone, but not to trust them the same way as you had previous to the offense. For example, if a friend stole $100 from you, that would be bad. Sometime later, they admit what they did, say they are truly sorry, and beg you to forgive them. You forgive them. Are you still going to trust them? No, that will take some time. It is possible that you will never trust them the same way again.

Forgiveness is simply letting it go. Forgiveness is the key to letting yourself out of jail. Just let it go. You don't forgive them because they deserve it. (They don't.) You forgive them for your benefit. It's counterproductive to harbor resentment and think that it is hurting the other person. It only hurts you.

I have had numerous people wrong me in my life. I have trusted people who turned out to be unworthy of my trust. It has not been easy to forgive them, to let it go. I have struggled at times, but I learned to let it go.

My faith is what enabled me to let it go. I am a Christian. God has forgiven me of all my sins. I should be an expert at forgiveness. I understand that since God has forgiven all my sins, I should forgive others who have offended me. Think about it: God forgave all my anger, lies, lust, covetousness, selfishness, etc. I want to be an expert at forgiveness. If you step on my toe, I am going to forgive you. It's just not that big of a deal. It's not worth keeping me in the prison of bitterness.

You might say, "Hey, Coach, you don't understand. You don't know what they did to me." You are right. I don't know. But I do know that anger and bitterness are a jail I have spent time in before, and I don't ever want to go back. Follow the advice given in the movie *Frozen*: let it go.

When you refuse to forgive, you are the prisoner and the jailer. Let yourself out. It's up to you.

DISCUSSION QUESTIONS

1. Why is it so hard to forgive people who have wronged you?

2. Would you be willing to share a time when you forgave someone who wronged you?

3. What does the fact that God has forgiven you mean to you?

4. How do you benefit from forgiving others?

BIBLE PASSAGE FOR ADDITIONAL STUDY

Matthew 18:23–35

PRINCIPLES OF FRIENDSHIP I

"Friendship is always a sweet responsibility,
never an opportunity."
—Khalil Gibran

"Iron sharpeneth iron;
so a man sharpeneth the countenance
of his friend."
—Proverbs 27:17

How important do you think your friends are? We are going to start a series of lessons dealing with the importance of friends and friendships.

This life lesson comes from death row. It was 1989, and our family had just moved from Lima, Ohio, to Chattanooga, Tennessee. After I came home from teaching school, I was retrieving our mail, and in the mailbox was a large manila envelope from a coaching friend who lived in Ohio. I was intrigued to see what would be in the envelope. It contained several newspaper articles. I assumed the articles would be sports-related. I was wrong.

The first article had a headline that said, "LIMA MAN WANTED IN TRI-STATE MANHUNT." I looked at the guy's picture but didn't read the first article. The second article said something like, "KILLER STILL AT LARGE." The third article once again had a picture of the suspect, and it said, "$10K REWARD FOR . . ." When I looked back at the picture, I recognized that the suspect was a former student of mine, who for this story we will call X.

I quickly went back to the first article and read every word of all four of the articles that were included in the envelope. It told how X had shot and killed his next-door neighbor. He took some jewelry and electronics. He then took her car and fled to Toledo, Ohio, to hide out with friends.

While X took a nap, his friends heard a news bulletin on the TV offering a $10,000 reward for any information that would lead to his arrest and conviction. They called the police and X was taken into custody. It was very possible that X would face the death penalty. He was taken by the authorities back to Allen County. He would be in the jail in Lima until his trial.

I first met X when he was in sixth grade. He was a rowdy but likable kid. He came from a very well-to-do family. His dad owned a well-known company that employed many people in Allen County. I coached X in middle school baseball. I taught him Ohio history in seventh grade and US history in eighth grade.

I remember X was a little insecure. He not only wanted people to like him, he *needed* for people to like him. He often bought pizza or Cokes for classmates, in an attempt to win their friendship. In those days, it was hard to find left-handed golf clubs. X bought a set of left-handed golf clubs for his soccer coach as a Christmas present. What I am saying is that he wasn't a bad person. He was thoughtful. He was generous. You would have enjoyed being his classmate.

At the beginning of ninth grade, X left our school to go to a larger school because he wanted to play big-time football. At that point, I lost track of X for six or seven years. We moved to Tennessee, and I never expected to see him again.

I called my friend, Mike, who had sent me the articles. We both had coached X and taught him in class. Mike thought I would want to know what happened, and he was right. He told me that X was in the Allen County Jail. I asked if it would be possible to visit X in jail, but he didn't know.

I called the Allen County Jail to see if it would be possible to visit with X. The guy on the other end of the line told me that I could not visit with him because he wasn't speaking to any reporters. I told him I was not a reporter, but he didn't believe me. He said no one would drive from Tennessee unless they were a reporter looking for a story. He said no one could visit X unless they were on his approved list of visitors. I told him I had been X's teacher and coach. I asked if he could see if X would put me on the approved list so I would be able to visit him. He said he had to take X some supper and he would ask him if he wanted to put me on his visitor list. I told him to ask X if he would be willing to speak to Coach T., because I wasn't sure he would know my name, but I was pretty sure he would remember me as Coach T. The guy said to call back in about ninety minutes and he would let me know if X put me on the list.

When I called back, the guy at the jail said X remembered me and added me to his visitor list. We talked about visiting hours and what I could bring into the jail. I was anxious to go and see X face-to-face. I took a personal day that Friday and drove seven hours to see X. We would have exactly sixty minutes to talk.

I went to the Kmart in the Eastgate Shopping Center and picked up a ten-pack of Big Red chewing gum and eight Snickers bars. I also had a Bible to give to X. I went to the Allen County Courthouse, where I was searched. Even though I would only be at the jail for an hour, it was still intimidating to hear those doors slam shut behind me. I went into a small room and sat down at a table. At precisely four p.m., the door opened and X walked in. He smiled pleasantly and said it was good to see me. I said that I wished it were under different circumstances, and he quickly agreed. We talked about how his family was holding up, and he thanked me for the chewing gum, candy bars, and the Bible.

We spent about the next thirty minutes talking about his eternal destiny. I was concerned about him and his never-dying soul. It was a good talk. I had underlined some verses and written the references in the back of the Bible that I gave him. He promised to read all of the verses later that night.

I then asked X if he would forgive me. I told him I try really hard to reach all the students in my classes. It was obvious to me that I hadn't helped him. I had failed him. Maybe if I had been better prepared or maybe if I had worked harder I could've reached him. I told him I was sorry for my shortcomings and asked for his forgiveness. He said he would not forgive me. I was surprised because the X I knew wasn't really like that. After a short pause, he said, "You don't need to be forgiven. You get forgiveness when you have done something wrong. I can't forgive you because you didn't do anything wrong. You taught us. You cared about us, I know that. Didn't you teach us something like you can make choices but you don't get to choose what happens after that? Didn't you teach us that we have to take total responsibility for ourselves? I don't forgive you, because it's my fault that I'm in this situation, not your fault."

Even though X said that, I still felt a sense of failure that I hadn't reached him. It still haunts me to this day that he sat in my classroom, heard all that I had to say, and ended up taking another person's life.

The time was flying by, and our hour would soon be up. I said, "X, what happened to you? How do you go from a happy-go-lucky middle school kid to death row?" He said, "When I went to my new school, I fell in with a rough bunch of guys. I wanted them to like me. I always had plenty of cash, and I tried to buy their friendship. It started out with beer, then it was weed, and before I knew it, I was using harder stuff. I got addicted to crack and started low-level dealing to support my own habit.

"When I needed some money for drugs, I knew where to get it. Our next-door neighbor always went to get her hair fixed on Friday morning so it would look good for church on Sunday. When our neighbors went on vacation, I always fed their dog, got their mail, and brought in the newspapers. I had done this for years since I was a little kid. I knew all the codes to their security system. I waited for her to leave, entered the codes, and quickly went inside. I gathered up a couple of TVs and some other electronics. I also got quite a bit of jewelry, which I knew I could unload quickly.

"I was just about to leave when I looked up and she was standing there staring at me. She said, 'What are you doing here?' I said, 'I'm robbing you.' She said, 'Please don't hurt me, X! Please. I have known you all your life. I brought a teddy bear over the day you came home from the hospital right after you were born. Please don't hurt me.'"

He told her he was not going to hurt her. He said he would tie her up but that she would be fine. He told her to go to a corner of the room and kneel down with her hands behind her back. He said he was going to duct tape her hands behind her back, but the gun went off by accident. He swore it was an accident, but I didn't believe it.

Let's get real. If we went hunting and you shot me by accident, the chances are you would hit me in the armpit or in the behind or blow off my big toe. It could happen that you accidentally hit me with a kill shot, but if it were a random shot, the chances are great that I would recover from the wound.

I was a little upset. I had driven seven hours to have a guy look me in the eye and lie to my face. He swore up and down that it was an accident. He was emphatic that he had no intention of hurting her in any way. I just didn't think that his story was believable. I still don't believe it.

The jailer yelled, "Five minutes. You got five minutes! Wrap it up." I told X that I would be standing in front of 140 students in my classes on the following Monday. If he were to speak to my students, what would he say? If he could be in my classroom, what advice would he have for each of them? He never hesitated. He said, "That's easy; I'd tell them: your friends can make you or break you. I wouldn't be here if I hadn't followed, like a sheep, a group of people who didn't care about me one bit. Tell 'em to watch who their friends are."

Life lesson number seventeen comes from death row.

> **Your friends can make you or break you.**

If X were to come and visit your home today, that's what he'd tell you. It's pretty good advice.

DISCUSSION QUESTIONS

1. Why is it harder to say no to a friend than just some random person?

2. Can you tell us about something you have done that you shouldn't have either to make a friend or keep a friend?

3. Has a friend ever asked you to do something that was either immoral or unethical?

4. Would you lie to a friend's parent to help a friend cover their tracks?

BIBLE PASSAGE FOR ADDITIONAL STUDY

II Samuel 13:2–15

PRINCIPLES OF FRIENDSHIP II

"Friendship consists of forgetting what one gives
and remembering what one receives."

—Alexander Dumas

"He that walketh with wise men shall be wise:
but a companion of fools shall be destroyed."

—Proverbs 13:20

H ave you ever noticed how little kids are copycats? They watch everything older people do, whether it's their older sibling or parent. They will copy the way their older brother sits or holds their hand on their chin, or whatever. Can you think of an example of something you have seen your little brother or sister or a niece or nephew copy?

I was walking at the back of the church on a Wednesday night in 1985. The service was over. I was carrying my little girl, and my oldest son was walking beside me. My wife was in the nursery with our youngest boy. Our pastor asked if he could speak to me for a minute. I said sure. He asked if I still painted houses in the summertime. I told him I did. He said one of the ladies in our church was elderly, and that she needed to get her house painted. It was a two-story house not far from our house. He gave me her number, and I said I would go and see her the next day when I got out of school.

The next day, I went to see her at her home. Her name was Mrs. D. She was in her mid-eighties and very alert. I really enjoyed meeting her and told her we would get her house taken care of. She was very concerned about how the paint was weathered and peeling. Ohio winters are very tough on paint jobs. She mentioned that she had always painted in the past but that she wouldn't be able to at this time because she was blind in one eye after her attack.

After her attack! She just stated it matter-of-factly, like it was no big deal. I didn't know anything about her attack. I had not heard about that. I asked her when she was attacked and she told me it was in the middle of September, the year before.

Our youngest son, Mitch, was born on September 9, 1985. He spent the first five weeks of his life in the intensive care unit at the Medical College of Ohio Hospital. He had many surgeries and procedures during this time. After six weeks, we were able to take him home. That entire time was a blur. It was as if someone had hit the fast-forward button on our lives. Everyone in our church was well aware of what had happened to Mrs. D. Everyone except us, that is. We were so concerned about our child that we had no time for newspapers or to watch the news on TV.

I told Mrs. D. that we were not aware of what had happened to her. I asked her what had happened. She said she was upstairs reading her Bible when she heard some noise downstairs in the kitchen. She slipped halfway down the stairs and saw a flashlight shining in her kitchen. Someone was looking for something to steal. When she went to go back upstairs, the wooden step creaked loudly. The intruder started coming toward her. She ran to the phone in her room. It was an old rotary phone, not a push-button phone like we have today. This being the case, it would take longer to call the police. She was halfway through dialing the numbers when the attacker ripped the phone from her hand and began beating her in the face with it. He hit her fifteen or twenty times with such force that her left eye was detached and lying on her cheek. He then took a butcher knife from her kitchen and stabbed her in the shoulders and chest repeatedly. She showed me faint scars from where he had attempted to cut her nose off of her face. Her eyeball was on her cheek and her nose flopped over her mouth and rested on her chin. Before she lost consciousness, she looked up and saw her attacker.

I was absolutely stunned. I asked Mrs. D. if the police caught the animal that had done that to her. She nodded and her lip started to quiver. A big tear slowly rolled down the right side of her face. She said in a low whisper, "It was my grandson" (who we will call J). My heart sank as I saw all the pain in her face as she relived those horrible moments. I just stood there with tears streaming down my face. I had no idea what to say.

"He was a good boy, Coach T.," she said. Actually, J was her great-grandson. Her granddaughter was extremely bright. I think she had taken the ACT test when she was thirteen years old and scored something like a 29 or 30. She was gifted and destined for great things. As she progressed in school, colleges and universities from all over the country were recruiting her. Ivy League schools, Stanford, Vanderbilt, and many others not only offered her a full academic scholarship but also a six or seven thousand dollar stipend to attend their school. Can you imagine that? Not only would she not have to pay to attend a school to which most of us never could be admitted, some schools were actually offering her money to choose them.

At seventeen years of age she got pregnant. Her mother was extremely angry with her. She berated her daughter and told her she was really stupid for somebody who was supposed to be so smart. She refused to help her daughter in any way at the time she needed help the most. Mrs. D. stepped in and told her granddaughter she was willing to help. She said, "You're a smart girl with a bright future, and you need to take advantage of the opportunities that you have." She agreed to take the child and raise him as her own. She told her granddaughter she could come back and get him anytime she desired in the future.

Her granddaughter went to the University of Cincinnati and graduated with a degree in electrical engineering. She went to Ohio State University in Columbus, Ohio, for further study. While working on a master's degree, she met and fell in love with an extremely sharp young man. Their relationship became very serious, and after several months they were contemplating marriage. She was fearful that if her boyfriend found out about her past he would lose interest in her, so she never told him about her son.

"He was a good boy, Coach T." I would guess she said that four or five times. I didn't say anything, but I wondered, if he was a good boy, what do bad boys do? Mrs. D. was really the only mother J had ever known. She took him to church every time the doors were open. She made sure he always had plenty to eat. She bought all of his clothes, toys, school supplies, and medicine. They had a close relationship for many years. She was so proud of the sweater she was wearing. It was a gift he had given her for her birthday. In her mind only a good boy would be thoughtful enough to purchase his grandma such a nice birthday gift.

He started running around with a rough crowd his last couple of years in high school. He started with alcohol and then progressed to dabbling with drugs. Before long, J forgot about all the sacrifices his grandmother had made for him over the years. He drifted away from her. "He became just like his friends. The boy I raised was not like that at all. He was thoughtful and kind. He was pleasant. He had a great sense of humor. I just enjoyed that child so much. But now he was a different person. He was just like them."

She said that Officer Ted had saved her life. I said, "Ted B.? From church?" She said yes. "He's the one who found me." I couldn't wait to talk to him and get more details. I knew him well. We attended the same Sunday school class at church.

When I saw Ted at church the next Sunday, I told him I had met a member of his fan club. He laughed and said he had so many members that he couldn't keep up with all of them. I told him that I had met Mrs. D. and was going to paint her house. He looked down at the top of his shoes and said he wasn't very proud of that police work. I was confused, because Mrs. D. said that Ted had saved her life.

Ted told me that he was in his police car when the call went out for somebody to check on an elderly lady living on Oak Street. They gave her name and said the neighbors were concerned because they had not seen her out working in her yard for a couple of days. She always worked on her flowers. They were afraid that maybe she had fallen or maybe she had had a heart attack. They wanted the police to come by and check on her. Ted got on his radio and told the dispatcher that he knew Mrs. D. and he would be glad to check on her.

When Mrs. D. didn't respond to Ted's knock on her door, he took his tools, picked the lock, and let himself in. The house had been closed up for several days. The stench of dried blood was awful. He followed the smell up the stairs and found Mrs. D.'s body lying in a lake of blood on the floor. Ted was no rookie. He had been a police officer for more than twenty years but had never seen anything as gruesome as this. Ted was ashamed, but he said he never even checked for a pulse. He radioed for a funeral home to send someone to pick up Mrs. D.'s body. As he was asking, she groaned. He hurriedly changed the request for an ambulance. He could not believe she was still alive.

I can't remember now, but they put fourteen or sixteen units of blood into Mrs. D. She had so many wounds that the blood ran out of her as fast as they could put it in. Somehow she had survived for almost forty-eight hours before she was found. Other than being completely blind in her left eye, Mrs. D. made a remarkable physical recovery, but I doubt she ever recovered from the emotional pain of that traumatic evening.

Life lesson eighteen is: *You become just like your friends.* I am not saying that if you have bad friends, you will try to kill your grandma. I'm sure this is a very extreme case. But what I am saying is that you will become like your friends. Since that is the case, it is very important that you take a lot of care when choosing who your friends will be. We get advice from our friends. We listen to our friends. We start to think like our friends. We take on their values. You become just like your friends.

> **Let's make sure that our friends are good people who will steer us in the right direction.**

DISCUSSION QUESTIONS

1. Are there any phrases you have picked up from your friends?

2. What are some things that your friends could pressure you to do that are either dangerous or wrong?

3. How will others view you in light of the friends you have?

4. In what ways can good friends have an impact on you?

BIBLE PASSAGE FOR ADDITIONAL STUDY

I Samuel 23:15–29

PRINCIPLES OF FRIENDSHIP III

"There is nothing better than a friend,
unless it is a friend with chocolate."
—Linda Grayson

"But Amnon had a friend . . ."
—11 Samuel 13:3

I was sound asleep in bed when the phone rang. It was about 3:30 a.m., and I assumed the worst. People don't normally call my house at 3:30 a.m. unless it is very bad news. I was in a fog when I heard a voice on the other end of the line say, "Coach, they are trying to kill me. I need you to come right now and get me. Hurry! This is serious!"

I asked, "Okay, first of all, who is this?" He said, "It's me, M." Then he gave his last name. He said, "Hurry, I don't have much time." I was wondering who the "they" who would be killers were. I also wondered if it would be really risky (not to mention dumb) to go and get between M and these assassins. To be honest, I just wanted to go back to sleep because I was still tired, and it would be inconvenient to get up and go. I was ready to give a lame excuse like, "Hey, I'd like to help out, but my cat is about to have puppies," or whatever. Anything that would get me off the hook! I heard him say, "Please, Coach. You are the only one I can think of to call. My dad is out of the state. I know you care about me. I know you won't let me down." I wasn't happy about it, but I pulled on a pair of jeans and some sneakers. My wife wasn't very pleased either. I just didn't want to read in the paper about M's death and know I did nothing to help him. He was one of my former players, and although I hadn't seen him for four or five years, I knew I needed to try to help if I could.

As I drove our rusty Corolla to the spot where he told me to pick him up, I tried to figure out who was trying to kill him. The police? A gang? An angry husband? This fiasco was really stupid, because I was literally and figuratively in the dark. And I was very scared. I thought about turning around several times. Who would I outrun in my old car? Let's face it: that car went 0 to 60 miles per hour in 5.9 days. The only way it could go 75 miles per hour was if it went off a cliff. And it would be our getaway car? Great plan, Coach!

I drove over and slowed down. He came running out of some bushes and dove into the backseat. Even though I knew he was going to do that, it was still kinda scary. He stayed low in the backseat and I drove all over the place. I wanted to be sure no one was following before I headed for home. Every time somebody followed us, I was convinced it was the bad guys. It never was, but I was so sure that we would never make it.

Finally, after I was convinced no one was following us, we went to our house in Rossville, Georgia. My wife got up and fixed breakfast and we ate as M caught us up on what he had done since leaving the school where I had coached him.

Actually, M didn't leave that school. He was not allowed to return for his senior year. On the last day of school of his junior year M thought it would be funny to walk around the school with a lit cigarette in his mouth. He went into two or three classrooms nonchalantly wishing the teachers a good summer vacation. This was a Christian school with many rules. They didn't think M was funny at all.

M thought, *It's the last day of school. What are they gonna do? It's not a big deal. Let's have some laughs. I'm a great athlete. They need me for basketball and baseball. They won't do anything to me.*

All of these thoughts turned out to be wrong. It was a big deal. It didn't matter that it was the last day of school. It didn't matter how many sports M played or how well he played them. He had to go by the same rules as everyone else.

I really think M thought we couldn't have a team without him. You need to understand that playing a sport on a school team is a privilege and not a right. We will have a team with or without you. If you play on our team it will be on our terms, not on yours. Putting on that uniform has responsibilities that need to be taken seriously.

At any rate, the teachers and the administration were ready for M to take his act somewhere else. It was unfortunate because I wanted to help M, but the school wasn't gonna have it. Finally, I made an appeal to our school administrator. I asked if M could come back on a zero-tolerance policy. No problems of any kind, at any time, with any teacher or student. No disruptions. No disrespect. Nothing! If M burped he would be gone—whether he said "excuse me" or not. Also, M would not be allowed to play sports. He could be the manager. He could pick up sweaty towels and hand out water to the team. He could come to practice, but he could not play. Even if he had a perfect first semester, he could not play basketball the entire year. This would allow me to work with M, and hopefully he would learn a tough lesson: we get to make choices, and those choices have consequences.

Our administrator prayed about my appeal and agreed M could come back. There would be no basketball for M. He could attend practices and games, but he could not play. Rumor had it that Coach T. was desperate to get M back in school and back on the team. I think M was telling people that, but I am not sure. Many people criticized me (behind my back) and said all I cared about was winning. It was really unfair, but that's how some people are. At no point was M going to play basketball for us, but some people just love to talk.

When M found out he could not play sports for us the next year, he enrolled at another school for his senior year. M was a very tough defender who wasn't a big scorer. He might make six or eight points a game. His value was on the defensive end of the floor. He was strong and determined. He loved the challenge of guarding an opposing team's best player and taking him out of the game. He would often hold a twenty-point scorer to six or eight points and totally frustrate them in the process. He had a way of putting good players on tilt.

His new coach was all about offense. They didn't really worry about defense. They just tried to outscore you. M got lost in the shuffle and saw his playing time would be minimal. So after going to a couple of camps with them, he decided to go to a third school. The third school was much like the second for M. They didn't see his value, and he felt like they didn't give him much of a chance. He eventually quit toward the end of the season as his playing time dwindled and his frustration mounted.

M came to our graduation to see all his old classmates get their diplomas. He was glad to see me and told me how he regretted his poor choices. I told him to stay on track because I still wanted him to live up to his potential.

M had a friend who helped him get a job at a gentlemen's club—a strip club. M was tough and liked to fight. If the drunks got too boisterous and rowdy, he showed them to the door.

After a few months at the club, M was offered an extra job. He would drive to Atlanta twice a week. He drove to the parking lot at Grant Field on the campus of Georgia Tech, parked the car, got in another car, and drove back to the club in Chattanooga. It was a four-hour job that would pay him $1,000 per trip. That's $250 per hour, ladies and gentlemen. If somebody offers you $250 an hour to do something, you can be sure it is probably not moral or legal. He was told never to exceed the speed limit and never to look in the trunk.

M made really good money for a couple of years. Unfortunately, he also wasted a lot of money living a fast, partying lifestyle. M had grown up in a good family. He knew right from wrong. But his friends had a greater influence on him than his family.

After going to a revival with his grandfather, M made a decision to quit his jobs. He would start living the way he knew was right. He tried to give his employer a two-week notice so they could get someone else.

You don't give a two-week notice to drug dealers. They aren't like Walgreen's. You can't quit them. You know too much. They had three or four guys rough him up and make it clear they would kill his mom and both of his sisters if he didn't show up for work.

After he got beat up, M was cleaning the blood off his face when one of the girls from the club warned him that she overheard the boss telling some guys that M couldn't be trusted anymore. They were gonna get rid of him. They had already slashed all of his tires so he couldn't leave. She told him to call someone to come get him. That's when he called me. Gee, thanks!

We made arrangements for M to go stay a few months with my in-laws. My wife's dad printed Christian literature and Bibles in Spanish to send to missionaries in Mexico and Central America. In the meantime, a Chattanooga detective friend would pay a visit to the club owner and let him know M was out of the state. The detective made it crystal clear that if anything happened to any of M's family, the police department would close the club and dig into their computers to find out just exactly what they were up to.

The police eventually raided the club and shut it down completely. Seven or eight years later, I ran into M. He owned three restaurants and was doing great. He and his wife now have three lovely children. They are truly blessed.

M's life was an absolute mess for several months. He came from a good family, but he associated with some really bad people. Those bad people influenced him to make some horrible choices that could have cost him his freedom and even his life.

> **Many times your friends will influence
> you more than your family.**

DISCUSSION QUESTIONS

1. Who is a family member you look up to and why?

2. Who is the most influential person in your life right now?

3. Have you ever been influenced by a friend to do something your parents would not approve of?

4. Tell us about a time when a friend influenced you to do something positive or something right.

BIBLE PASSAGE FOR ADDITIONAL STUDY

Mark 6:14–29

LIFE LESSON 20

PRINCIPLES OF FRIENDSHIP IV

"Friendship improves happiness, and abates misery,
by doubling our joys, and dividing our grief."
—Cicero

"A man that hath friends must show himself friendly:
and there is a friend that sticketh closer than a brother."
—Proverbs 18:24

Who is the best college basketball player you ever saw? I think Michael Jordan is probably the best pro player I've seen, because he made everybody on his team better. His confidence rubbed off on the other guys. He also played his best when it mattered most.

Jordan was not the best college player I ever saw. Len Bias of Maryland would hold that distinction. Bias was a better college player because he was a better shooter than Jordan, a more dominant rebounder than Jordan, and bigger and stronger than M.J. Len Bias was like Michael Jordan on steroids. He was six eight and weighed 210 pounds. He was one of the first basketball players to lift weights during the season. (Before this time it was thought by many that lifting weights during the season would throw off your shot.) He could score inside or outside. He was ultracompetitive and an unselfish team player. He led Maryland to its zenith in basketball honors as the Terps won the ACC Tournament. Bias was an All-American as well as the Atlantic Coast Conference's Player of the Year twice. He was the ACC Athlete of the Year for all sports in 1986. He had unparalleled athletic ability and size, yet he also had a tremendous knowledge of how to play the game. Bias was as fierce a competitor as you will ever see playing any sport as well.

On June 17 Bias was selected as the second overall pick in the 1986 NBA Draft by the defending NBA champion Boston Celtics. A new shoe company wanted Bias to be the face of their aggressive advertising campaign. They wanted to challenge industry giants Nike and Adidas. The new company was Reebok. Bias agreed to wear Reebok shoes exclusively and film three commercials for Reebok in exchange for $1.6 million over five years. He also would receive tens of thousands of dollars worth of Reebok shoes and gear for himself as well as his friends and family. (How great would that be? Free swag for all your friends! Free shirts, hoodies, sweatpants, hats, and shoes all around! You'd be like Santa Claus! "Just tell me your size and favorite color." Reebok might not be my favorite shoe, but let's be honest—I'd wear pink heels to school every day for $300K. If you laughed at me I'd hit you with my purse . . . and cry all the way to the bank. Three hundred thousand to wear shoes. Wow!)

Two days after the draft Bias went out to celebrate with some friends and teammates. His dad told him, "Be careful. Be careful what you do; be careful who you are with." Bias returned to his dorm in Washington Hall at three a.m. A long-time workout partner and friend, Brian Tribble, had some cocaine. He knew Bias didn't use drugs, but he figured Bias might be interested in trying it since they were celebrating. He warned Bias that this cocaine was very pure and very powerful. "I'm a horse, Trib. I can take it." But Bias couldn't take it; he had a seizure and collapsed around 6:25 a.m. At 6:32, when Tribble made the 9-1-1 call to get an ambulance, Bias was unconscious and not breathing. He was put on a ventilator to breathe for him, but all attempts at restarting his heart failed. He was pronounced dead at Leland Memorial Hospital in Riverdale, Maryland, at 8:55 a.m. The official cause of death was cardiac arrhythmia related to his cocaine use. He was twenty-two years of age.

Two former girlfriends and numerous teammates said they had never known of Bias ever to use drugs at any time. He took a lot of pride in maintaining his strength and conditioning. Three different NBA teams had tested him prior to the draft, and there was no trace of drugs in his system. Keith Gatlin, Bias's friend and teammate, stated that he had been to Bias's home, had been with him year-round for three years, and had taken him to his home in North Carolina, but had never once seen Bias use drugs of any kind. Bias had never used drugs prior to June 18.

His family got no money from the Celtics. He never played a game for them. They got no money from Reebok. He never shot a commercial for them. He gave up his future because of a person he thought was his friend.

Nobody had a brighter future than Len Bias. He had unmatched athletic gifts, an amazing work ethic, and the competitive drive of an assassin. His magnetic personality and humble demeanor would attract endorsement jobs from major corporations like moths to a flame.

But Len Bias had a friend. That friend, Brian Tribble, was a drug dealer who later served ten years in prison for drug trafficking.

Four days after Bias's death, more than eleven thousand people attended his memorial service at Cole Field House, where he had starred for the University of Maryland. His death was a shock to the nation. I still remember where I was when I heard Len Bias had died.

Len Bias lost his life at age twenty-two. I would guess at least $250 million in future earnings and endorsements were lost. He is not remembered for all the great things he achieved and all the ability he had been blessed with. He is remembered for the dumbest thing he ever did. He made a bad choice, and it cost him his life. *Choose friends who will be lifters who will encourage you to greater heights.* This is crucial, because your future might depend on your friends. We will never know what great things Len could have accomplished had he not had a friend named Brian Tribble.

Four Principles of Friendship
1. Your friends can make you or break you.
2. You are or will become just like your friends.
3. Many times your friends will influence you more than your family.
4. Your future could depend on your friends.

DISCUSSION QUESTIONS

1. What are some choices you could make that would negatively impact your future?

2. Are the choices you are making now going to get you where you want to go in life?

3. How can your current friends be a positive influence on you and your future?

4. What could you do to have a positive impact on your friends' futures?

BIBLE PASSAGES FOR ADDITIONAL STUDY

Proverbs 12:26
Proverbs 13:20

EVERYONE PREACHES THEIR OWN MEMORIAL

"When I stand before God at the end of my life,
I would hope that I would not have
a single bit of talent left,
and could say, 'I used everything you gave me.'"
—Erma Bombeck

"A good name is rather to be chosen
than great riches . . ."
—Proverbs 22:1

Stephen Covey gave this very fitting illustration in his book *The Seven Habits of Highly Effective People.* Imagine you are getting dressed to go to a memorial service. You put on your best clothes. It is a serious occasion.

The memorial is to be held at our gym. It can seat about two thousand people. The place is packed, and there is nowhere to park without walking a great distance.

When you get inside you see friends, family members, classmates, teammates, teachers, church members, and neighbors. They are there to pay respect to the family and to support them in a time of sorrow. They want to celebrate the life that was lived. They will share stories that will give people a sense of the type of person the deceased was.

Before taking a seat you pick up a program from a table in the lobby. The front simply says "MEMORIAL SERVICE." On the inside it has your picture. *It's your memorial service!* You are invisible. That's why they didn't speak to you or hand you a program when you went in.

Six people are going to speak at the memorial service. Let's say this service is going to take place twenty-five years from now. None of us know how long we will live. But just to simplify things, let's say twenty-five years from today your memorial service would be held. What will you want those six people to say? How could you get them to say nice things about you when you are gone?

I've actually thought a lot about my memorial service. I would want people to remember and celebrate the life I lived. I wouldn't want them to high-five the fact that I was gone, but I would want them to laugh and remember moments we had shared. Or maybe tell some way that I encouraged them or helped them on their journey. Or remind people that I cared about them or was proud of them.

If my boss spoke I'd want him to say I was a dependable worker who cared about the kids. I'd want him to say he wished he had a hundred more teachers just like me.

I'd want my coworkers to say I was great to work with. I was positive and supportive. I would help them any way I could. I would want them to say if they ever needed help they called on me first. I was their go-to guy in time of need.

I'd want my pastor to say I was faithful. I would want him to say I was a servant. I'd want him to say I was generous. Do you think my pastor would get up and lie to people at my memorial? No, he would never lie. Ever! His character wouldn't allow him to do that. So if I want him to say those things about me, what do I have to do? I have to start today and be faithful. I can't just attend church on Christmas and Easter and skip the rest of the time. I have to be a servant.

A couple of years ago on a Sunday night our pastor asked if I could watch the cars in the parking lot and help a couple of little old ladies get in their cars after the service. The guy they had scheduled for parking lot duty was sick that night and they needed a volunteer. Could I help?

I told him I couldn't for two reasons: 1) I come to church to hear good preaching and to hear people sing and bring glory to God, not to guard cars, and 2) I'm Coach T. I'm kind of a big deal. I'm way too important to be out there helping old ladies get in church and parking their cars. Get some kid to do that.

Do you really think I told him that? Of course not. I told him I'd be glad to serve in any way they needed me. Just whistle and I will come running. Currently I teach an adult class, but if they asked me to teach ten-year-old boys instead, I'd give it my best. I want him to say, "Coach T. was a servant of the Lord." He's not gonna say that if I'm prideful and lazy.

It would be disappointing to me if one of my former students got up and said I was awesome. It really would. That is not what I would want them to leave my classroom with. I want them to say, "Coach T. thought *we were awesome.* He believed in us. He cared about us. He thought we could accomplish amazing things." That would really be cool. I have no doubt that I believe in my students more than they believe in themselves.

I would want my friends to say I was an encourager and that I was supportive. I'd want them to say I was unselfish and generous, the kind of guy who would do you a favor and never keep score on who drove to the golf course last time or whatever. I'd want them to say I was so happy to celebrate their success and I was a person to turn to if you needed an encouraging word or a listening ear.

I wouldn't want my daughter to talk about how many games my teams won or how many times I was named Coach of the Year. That's not the relationship we have. I'm her dad. I'd want her to remember when I taught her to drive a stick shift or laughs we had on family vacations. I'd want her to talk about how much I believed in her, how proud I was of her, and how much I loved her and our family.

How can I be sure that she talks about those things? The only way is for me to make sure she knows that I believe in her today. I need to let her know that I am proud of her today. I need to demonstrate great love to her and our family today.

If I want my wife to say that I am hopelessly in love with her, I have to demonstrate my genuine love every day. I need to be thoughtful, considerate, and patient every day. She really is amazing. She knows my many flaws better than anyone, yet she still loves and believes in me. I need to tell her every day how much I treasure her company. She needs to know how thankful I am to have her in my life. Daily!

We don't know how many years we have left. Most people think some preacher will get up and preach their memorial services. In reality, we all preach our own memorial service by the way we live our lives.

In early January 2014, a dear friend of mine had a massive heart attack and died. He and his wife were friends to us at one of the toughest times of our lives. He always thought about others first. He cared about all people. He stood strong without apology for what he believed. At the same time, Marc was never judgmental. Heaven became a lot more real to us after Marc died. He's in God's hands, but he'll be in our hearts forever.

A unique part of Marc's memorial service was a six-and-a-half-minute clip of him preaching to his church . . . and everyone there. His message was, "We can't quit." No one there will ever forget it.

> **Live your life one day at a time.**
> **Let people know how important they are to you.**
> **Preach your own memorial service**
> **by the way you live today.**

DISCUSSION QUESTIONS

1. How do you want to be remembered by your family, friends, teammates, or coworkers?

2. What can you do today to shape how you will be remembered?

3. What changes do you need to make in your everyday life to ensure that you leave the legacy you hope to have?

4. Tell us about a family member whose memory inspires you as you look to your own future.

BIBLE PASSAGE FOR ADDITIONAL STUDY

Proverbs 22:1

IT'S HARD TO RUN A RACE IN A RAINCOAT

"The good is the enemy of the best."
—Anonymous

"Lay aside every weight . . ."
—Hebrews 12:1

The Olympic Games are only held once every four years. The whole world watches. My family always enjoys the Olympics greatly. My wife really enjoys the gymnastics. I enjoy the boxing, because the matches are really short. They only fight four rounds, so the fighters can't just dance around the ring, cautiously avoiding one another. The scoring tends to reward the aggressor, so the fighters really mix it up. I also enjoy the contrasting styles and tactics of the fighters. Asians approach the ring differently from Western Europeans, and American fighters' styles contrast with those from Eastern Europe.

The events I enjoy the most, though, are track-and-field events. I enjoy the high jump, the long jump, the relays, and the sprints. I love the 100-meter race. We give the label "world's fastest man" to the guy who can cover the 100-meter the fastest. In the 2012 London Olympics, Jamaican sprinter Usain Bolt set a new Olympic record by running a 9.63 100-meter. It was the second-fastest time ever. (He already had a world record by running the 100-meter in 9.58 seconds in a non-Olympic event.)

The *London Daily Mail* newspaper estimated the global TV audience who watched the twenty-five-year-old "Lightning Bolt" repeat his gold-medal-winning performance in front of two billion people. Bolt is fast and he's famous. And I could beat him in a 100-meter race. I'm sure of it.

I'm closer to sixty years old than fifty. I've never been called fast by anyone, ever, in my life. I never run. I walk daily, but I *never* run. I tell my students that if they see me running, they are to immediately call the police. Someone must be chasing me—that's the only way I'm running anywhere.

There is a circumstance that would allow me to beat the great Usain Bolt in a 100-meter sprint. He has covered this distance in just more than nine and a half seconds. How could I be so sure that I could beat Bolt in a race?

Picture this in your mind. It's a race between a pale, unmuscular grandpa and one of the finest athletic specimens ever to compete on a track anywhere. He has had great coaching, great training, and the best nutrition. I walk out on the track and the crowd snickers. When I take off my sweats, they laugh out loud.

Bolt comes out in a huge rain slicker with a big floppy rain hat and gigantic galoshes. The huge boots he's wearing have large leaden inserts in the sole of each boot. He can hardly lift his feet. He can't beat anyone—even me—while weighted down with such heavy gear.

Have you ever seen the gear track athletes wear? They wear the lightest shoes possible. The singlet that they wear for a shirt is sleeveless and paper-thin, and their shorts are not long like basketball shorts. Runners don't worry about being in style. They want as little as possible to hold them back. They never have a sleeve flapping in the wind, offering them resistance. They are streamlined. Many even wear spandex to run in a race.

Nobody gets on the track and takes their mark with a raincoat on. Nobody backs into the starting blocks while wearing galoshes. That stuff will weigh you down, and it can even cost you the race. *It's hard to run a race in a raincoat.* That's life lesson number twenty-two.

I've alluded to it earlier and I'll talk more about it later, but life is not fair. It is often challenging. It can be difficult and dangerous. Sometimes it is nearly impossible. It is imperative that we get in the race with no extra weight.

> **What can weigh you down and prevent
> you from running your best?**

Anger and bitterness can weigh you down. They prevent you from running your best. Many poor attitudes can be lead weights that stop you cold. Some are: selfishness, pride, a sense of entitlement, apathy, and a victim mentality. All will serve as hurdles on your trek to the finish line. The same can be said of poor work habits (also known as laziness), blaming others, and excuse making.

Poor friends can be a major hindrance in running your race. You may have to leave some of your current friends behind if they are trying to get you off course or are placing obstacles in your lane. You have to keep your eye on the finish line. You can't be distracted by other things—even good things—if you are going to bring home the gold medal.

> **"Let us lay aside every weight . . . and let us run with patience the race that is set before us."**
> **—Hebrews 12:1**

The Apostle Paul ran a pretty impressive race. He understood how to win the race. You get rid of anything that weighs you down.

You don't run a race in a raincoat.

DISCUSSION QUESTIONS

1. What are some weights that could hinder you as you run your race?

2. What are some things you can do to get rid of the weights that are holding you back from winning your race in life?

3. Is your attitude going to lead you to success? If not, what changes could you make to improve your chances of success?

4. What must you do to train for running the race well in your spiritual life?

BIBLE PASSAGE FOR ADDITIONAL STUDY

Hebrews 12:1–2

THE 7UPS

"The world is run by those who show up."
—Robert B. Johnson

"Procrastination is the grave in which
opportunity is buried."
—Anonymous

L et's get this straight: I am a Coca-Cola man. Always
have been and don't see any need to change now.
In the next few chapters we are going to talk about
education, so I want you to picture a can of 7UP. I hope this
will prove helpful to those of you who are in school or who
have kids (or grandchildren) who are in school. The 7UPs are
a formula for academic success. Nobody wants to struggle in
the classroom, but you have to follow the recipe to get the
best result. Just like you can't bake a delicious cake with rotten
eggs and spoiled milk, you can't skip crucial habits yet get an

education that will equip you to thrive in the future. Follow the 7UPs like an architect follows a blueprint, and you'll see results in the classroom.

Wake Up

You need to be rested and ready to learn. Let's keep it very simple—*go to bed at a decent hour.* Get your rest. There is no way you can be your best in the classroom when you were up until 2:30 a.m. playing *Call of Duty.* Hey, I'm glad you were there to defend our freedom (while sitting on the sofa, staring at a big-screen TV, and eating Cheetos). That's fun. I get it. But there is no way you can be mentally sharp if you are not alert. When I stay up late to watch a ballgame on Saturday night, I doubt if my Sunday school lesson is all that sharp. I know it is also much harder for me to get all that I should from the sermon. That's not the preacher's fault. It's my fault. When I go to bed earlier, I am able to think much more clearly and process information better.

Show Up

Almost all the students who failed my class over the years could have easily passed had they just shown up. It's been said that 80 percent of life is just showing up. That sounds a little high, but you get the point.

Sit Up

Sit at the front of the classroom. You can see more clearly. You can hear better. You will be much less tempted to get off task if the teacher is just a few feet away and looking right at you. You are much more likely to be distracted if you sit at the back of the room. You wonder what the text somebody got was about. You wonder what they are texting back. You wonder what that girl four rows up was thinking when she did that to her hair. You read the T-shirts of the people in front of you. Your mind can find a dozen things to wander off and think about.

When you sit up front it will be much easier to stay locked in and engaged with the speaker. Sitting up front is where we want to be at the ballgame. We pay a lot more money for the best seats in the house. Take it from a guy who has sat in the nosebleed seats at the Final Four. You get a lot more out of the experience when you can actually see the players. I love the atmosphere and electricity at a Buckeye football game, but it is a much better experience with a better view of the action. Sit up front.

Listen Up

Take good notes. If you sat behind me at church you'd think I was writing a letter. I write almost nonstop. It keeps me focused. It helps me avoid distractions. I am so quick to think about other things if I don't lock in. The preacher says, "Number one—be faithful," and I write it down. If I don't write it down my mind can just wander off. I wonder who the Bengals are playing that day. Oh yeah, the Bears in Chicago. I wonder if we will get the game on TV. I wonder what we are having for lunch. Maybe roast beef. I thought I smelled roast as I was leaving the house. I wonder if all the kids and the grandchildren are coming over for lunch. I wonder if Josh saw the Buckeyes play yesterday. I wonder what time Mitch gets off work. By the time I come back the preacher is saying, "Number five is . . ." I just totally missed two, three, and four! So I take notes to stay on track.

Another way to listen up is to be an active listener. Ask questions if you are not sure what the speaker means. Ask yourself if you agree with what the speaker is saying, and you will find your mind wandering a lot less.

Keep Up

The classes I had trouble with were usually classes that I didn't enjoy. I wasn't engaged. I didn't ask questions. I got behind. *Do not get behind!* This is probably the most important of the 7UPs. Keep up! When you get way behind in a class, it is much easier to find yourself considering giving up. (Giving up is *not* one of the 7UPs.) Don't fall behind. It is easy to be overwhelmed if you are way behind. Let me illustrate.

When our grandson Asa was about three, he stayed with us one afternoon. For some reason, he had a need to get every toy out. He had puzzles, cars, farm animals, dinosaurs, blocks, games, and books everywhere. When his mother came to get him, she told him to clean up all the toys. He was overwhelmed. His lip quivered and he said he could never clean up all that stuff. I told him I would help. He picked up the red, blue, and yellow blocks. I picked up the green, orange, and purple ones. He got the dinosaurs, I got the farm animals. We eventually got it cleaned up by working together and reducing the huge job into several smaller tasks. It would have been much simpler to put together a puzzle and then put it away. Read a couple of books, put them up. That's just not how kids think. They want to get all the stuff out.

If you don't keep up, it is easy to feel like your situation is hopeless. The same could be said about your finances or your relationships. Falling behind complicates life and leads to frustration. Keep your life simple. Don't get behind.

Cowboy Up

According to Urban Dictionary, the term *cowboy up* means, "When things are getting tough you have to get back up, dust yourself off, and keep trying." You grit your teeth, accept the challenge, and do what it takes to finish the job! Some jobs are tougher than others. Just find a way to get the job done.

Don't fuss about how tough the class is or how you'll "never use this stuff in real life." Don't whine about how demanding the teacher is. Jon Gordon says that "complaining causes you to focus on everything but doing your best." Roll up your sleeves and do what needs to be done.

Snug Up

If you find yourself behind, the temptation is to avoid the teacher and deny you have a problem. Often the teacher says something like, "Susie, I need to see you after class for just a minute." Teachers want to help. They want to remind you about a test you need to make up or an essay that you need to rewrite.

The bell rings. The teacher is talking to another student, so Susie slips out of the room and doesn't check in with the teacher. What message does the teacher get? The teacher assumes Susie doesn't care. Many teachers figure, *If Susie doesn't care about her grade, why should I care? Hey, it's one less paper to grade.*

The teacher gets paid the same whether you turn in your work or not. If your teacher scolds you, it means they care about you. They give a rip. Be grateful. Don't duck and dodge the teachers that want to help you. If you spend a little extra time before or after class, they will get the message that you want to learn. They will see that your future matters to you. They will try even harder to help you learn.

The 7UPs are a sound game plan for academic progress. Follow the formula for success in the classroom and your future gets brighter. (And when you get thirsty, remember: things go better with Coke!)

DISCUSSION QUESTIONS

1. Which of the 7UPs is the greatest challenge for you and why?
2. Which of the 7UPs is the greatest strength for you and why?
3. What grade would you give yourself for following this formula for academic success and why?
4. What specifically can you do to improve your chances for academic success?

BIBLE PASSAGES FOR ADDITIONAL STUDY

I Corinthians 13:11
Colossians 3:23

WHO'S RESPONSIBLE?

"Parents can only give good advice
or put them on the right paths,
but the final forming of one's character
lies in their own hands."
—Anne Frank

"The ultimate folly is to think that
something crucial to your welfare
is being taken care of for you."
—Robert Brault

Who do you think is most responsible for your education?
- Your teachers?
- Your principal?
- Your parents?
- Your grandparents?
- The school board?

- The state government?
- The federal government?
- All of the above?
- None of the above?

Okay, the question might be a little misleading, but ultimately, none of these are as responsible for your education as you are.

We have six grandchildren. We are so proud of every one of them. They add so much joy to our lives. We want them to have great futures and contribute to society. We want them to love God and serve others.

We feel a responsibility to encourage them in their educational pursuits. We buy them books. We check their homework at times. We practice the spelling words, even those tricky sight words. We read to them and have them read to us. They think learning is fun, and we don't want them to lose that feeling. We feel a responsibility to help them climb the mountain of their education.

Their parents buy books for them and go to school programs. They help them with science and geography projects. They meet with the teachers and want to be informed if the teacher has concerns or problems. They support, encourage, prod, and maybe even threaten the kids to do their best at all times at school.

I hope every teacher our grandchildren have takes their responsibilities seriously. I want our grandchildren to work hard, not just to say that they can pass the standardized tests. I want them to be challenged to think, solve, reason, discover, and learn the things they need to know to meet the challenges of the twenty-first century. I hope my grandchildren never have a teacher that doesn't fully understand the responsibility they have to help kids form a foundation of knowledge and character in their lives.

I hope the principals at each school see that the course of study pursued by our grandchildren is balanced and rigorous. I want them to be challenged. We want them to think, to learn, and to know how to apply what they learn to everyday situations.

What I am saying is this: a lot of people have a lot of responsibility when it comes to educating young people. I've taught for thirty-five years. As a Christian, I believe I will one day give an account for the way I used my abilities and my influence in the classroom. Teachers, parents, principals, grandparents, school boards, and the government all play a role in your education. But let's cut to the chase: *You will decide the quality of your education.* If you really want to play the saxophone, speak Spanish, or play basketball (or whatever), you will put in the time to be proficient at these things. You will sacrifice lesser things that are not as important (i.e., video games). You will study, get a tutor, hire a coach, go to camp, or search the Internet to get needed information. If you really want an awesome education, you will leave no stone unturned in your pursuit of excellence.

Yes, teachers and parents need to be supportive of your quest. But every student gets the education that he/she really wants. Again, we are back to choices.

What type of education will you choose?

DISCUSSION QUESTIONS

1. On a 1–10 scale, rate how much responsibility you have been taking for your education. Tell why you chose that.

2. What are some steps you can take to claim more responsibility for your education?

3. What can you do today to ensure you get the best education?

4. In your day-to-day spiritual life, what can you do to grow?

BIBLE PASSAGES FOR ADDITIONAL STUDY

Proverbs 28:13
II Corinthians 5:10

LIFE LESSON 25

DON'T SETTLE

"The greatest danger is not that our aim
is too high and we miss it,
but that it is too low and we reach it."
—Michelangelo

"Greater is He that is in you than
he that is in the world."
—I John 4:4

What are your three favorite restaurants? What do you like to eat, and why do you like to go to these restaurants?

My three favorite restaurants are Porkers in downtown Chattanooga, El Metate in Soddy Daisy, and Outback Steakhouse. Porkers is my favorite because the staff is so friendly and every bite of their food is always consistently great. I love the Miss Piggy special with double pork. I've often said that if you joined restaurants like people join churches, I would be a member at Porkers.

We also enjoy going to the Mexican restaurant in Soddy Daisy. I like the steak nachos.

Outback Steakhouse is a place where our family likes to go for special occasions. It's pretty expensive, so we don't get to go very often, but we really enjoy the blooming onion appetizer and a good steak. I like their bread with honey butter, and Outback's food is consistently tasty as well.

Let's pretend our school has a Teacher of the Month contest.

Let's pretend you are one of my students.

Let's say the office announces the winner of the Teacher of the Month and I won. (Obviously, I'd never be Teacher of the Month. We have so many great teachers, and I am unworthy to carry their book bags. I realize this. This is just an example, so play along with me here, okay?)

Anyway, I won! Maybe they weren't good at counting the votes, we don't know. The next day I went to announce which of my classes wins the title of Class of the Month. The class that wins gets out of school on Friday to go to Outback Steakhouse for a free meal. (I wanted to go to Porkers but they said it's too far.) Of course I would pick your class (as far as you know).

Outback is really nice. Their food is very good and they have a fun atmosphere. Everybody loves their bread and honey butter. The servers take our orders. Some get steaks, lobster, filet mignon, the Outback special with shrimp—you name it. The school is paying, so yeah, we want appetizers. "Bring us four blooming onions and four cheese fries." (After all, my favorite verse in the Bible is II Templeton 2:2: "If it's free, it's for me." Okay, that's not really the Bible. I was just checking to see if you are still with me.)

The servers are bringing sizzling steaks and more bread. I already have a loaf of bread in my pocket to take home for later. (What can I say? I really like that bread.) I see Alex got a huge porterhouse. Anna got the Outback special with shrimp. I can hardly wait for my sirloin, medium well, with a baked potato. I have my napkin tucked under my collar. I have my weapons in my hands. No salad needed here—I'm a carnivore. And lettuce might be good for me, so I'm not taking any chances.

All our students have their food and are digging in. The server comes to my table and she places in front of me . . . *a Happy Meal! What?*

I'm more than a little grouchy about this turn of events. It's about to get crunk up in here. We may have to take it outside and settle this. That's how I roll (unless the server is too big and mean-looking. If that's the case, I'd just talk to her). Let's just say I'm not happy. I'm the Teacher of the Month. I'm kind of a big deal. *A Happy Meal? Seriously?*

Let's be honest. There's a time and a place for a Happy Meal. The time is when I have a grandchild with me and the place is McDonald's.

I don't get to go to Outback very often. When we get Outback, we eat every bite of food that they bring us. It's too expensive to waste that food. If anything is left over, we get a box and take it home to eat later. It might be tomorrow's lunch or an evening snack. We get everything we pay for. We get our money's worth.

Don't settle for a Happy Meal education.

We established in lesson number twenty-four that *you decide which education you pursue.* I am begging you to get an Outback education. Get the best education we can give you. If you attend a private school, your parents pay tuition for your education. If you go to a public school, taxpayers in your school district pay for your education. Property owners pay taxes that support the schools in their district. My wife and I pay taxes to support the Soddy-Daisy schools. I always try to convince our students to please get our money's worth. Don't settle for less than the best.

Let me illustrate this again. Let's say we are going to lunch but my car needs gas. Let's say I stopped for gas and I went inside and gave them $40 to fill it up. Let's say it cost $38 to fill it up. Do you think I would go back inside and get my two dollars back? Of course I would. I want every drop of gasoline that I paid for, and I want my change.

Please don't settle for a Happy Meal education. Get an Outback-quality education. It's your future. It's your choice. Get the best. You'll be glad you did. Life is challenging at times, even if you are well educated and have a good job.

> **Invest in your own future by getting a great education. If you settle for a substandard education, it could cost you in the future.**

DISCUSSION QUESTIONS

1. What are some other areas in life in which people often settle for less than the best?

2. Why would you ever settle for less than the best?

3. What are some costs you may pay if you don't get the best education?

4. How do you think you could strive for the best in your everyday life today and also in the future?

BIBLE PASSAGES FOR ADDITIONAL STUDY

Hebrews 11:6

Jeremiah 29:11

CAN YOU BEAT ME?

"Luck is what happens when preparation
meets opportunity."

—Seneca

"Take time to prepare.
The physician buries his mistakes,
but the architect can only advise his client
to plant vines."

—Frank Lloyd Wright

Imagine you are a student in my class. Let's say everybody in your grade is automatically entered into a contest. There is no entry fee to join the contest. First prize in the contest is $25,000, second place pays $15,000, and everybody in the contest who can beat Coach T. wins $5,000. In order to win the contest, you have to chop down your tree before anyone else does. Everyone has a tree exactly the same size. I will give you an ax and you must use that ax to chop down

162

your tree. You cannot go to Ace Hardware and buy a chainsaw. You cannot call your Uncle Roy to bring over his chainsaw or another ax. There are no substitutions. You must use the ax that I give you.

Would you say $25,000 is a lot of incentive to win that contest? As a matter of fact, $5,000 is a lot of money. All you have to do to win $5,000 is to beat Coach T. Do you think you can beat me in this lumberjack contest? Although it sounds like I'm bragging, I must say that I don't think anybody can beat me. Boy, that sounds really cocky, doesn't it? I have never been a professional lumberjack. I have never gone to a lumberjack camp. I haven't really used an ax very much in my lifetime. But I can say with total confidence that I am 100 percent sure none of you can beat old Grandpa and win the prize.

Maybe you think you can beat me because you are stronger than me. You might have more experience. Some of you think you will win because you are younger and in better physical condition. Some of you may say you are more motivated, that the money means more to you than it does to me. These are all valid points. You have analyzed the situation well and have done a good job sizing up the competition.

How can I be so sure that I will win this contest? As a matter of fact, I will even give you a thirty-minute head start before I ever go out and swing my ax for the first time. You are out there working really hard. You are sweating profusely. Your hands are developing blisters and feeling sore. You have hit the tree dozens of times but made no progress. The reason is very simple. I gave all of you the dullest axes I could find.

None of these axes will cut room-temperature butter. You're going to be very frustrated.

You're going to be even more frustrated when I carefully walk out there holding an ax with the sharpest blade ever seen. It has been sharpened and sharpened until you could drop a hair on the edge and it would split in two. After about ten or twelve swings, the chips start to fly. And when I see the chips fly, I get even more motivated. I start working even harder. This would be very discouraging for you. Most would probably quit the contest.

You had a lot of advantages when the contest started. No one can dispute that. But it doesn't matter how much stronger, younger, hungrier, or in better shape you are if you are stuck with a dull ax. It's a no-win situation that you find yourself in.

Life lesson number twenty-six is *sharpen your ax*. The point of coming to school each day is not just to make it to the weekend. Going to school is an opportunity to learn, not a sentence to serve.

You're not just here to try to get a diploma so you can hold the piece of paper and tell a future employer, "Hey, look! I have this piece of paper that says I graduated from a very good school. You need to give me a good job. You need to give me a lot of money." The boss doesn't care about your piece of paper. The boss doesn't care about how motivated you are to get a paycheck. He or she wants to know what you bring to the table.

The boss wants to know what you do well. He or she will want to know if you can make change. Can you manage the store's inventory? Can you get along with your coworkers? They want to know if you know how to treat customers and take care of their needs. They want to know if you have computer skills. They want to see if you have a good attitude and a great work ethic. Your future boss is hoping that your education has taught you how to cope with problems and frustrations in a positive way. They will also want to know if you can handle success without becoming arrogant. They will want to see that you are punctual and that you know how to manage your time well. They want to know if you are honest and can be trusted.

You need a very sharp ax when you graduate from school. This is one reason why it is very important that you never cheat on any assignment. I don't care if we are talking about a quiz or a homework assignment. *Never cheat!* If you cheat you are only cheating yourself. You won't know anything. You will be the frustrated guy or gal who is out there swinging a very dull ax and making no progress at all. Even though you have that diploma, it won't take long for your boss to figure out that you have a dull ax.

Another reason not to cheat is that you want to *guard your reputation.* You don't want to be known as someone who has poor character and no integrity. The Bible is right on target when it says, "A good name is rather to be chosen than great riches." I would rather get a C in a class and still have my character than get an A, be known as a cheat, and not learn anything.

School is not a sentence to be served. It is an
opportunity to sharpen your ax. It is a chance to
think, to analyze, to compare, to contrast, and
to create. Grab a file and start sharpening.

Our sixteenth President of the United States knew
something about using an ax. Abe Lincoln was renowned
as a craftsman whose specialty was split-rail fences. (Teams
at Lincoln Memorial University in Harrogate, Tennessee,
are called the Railsplitters.) Lincoln said, "If I only had six
hours to chop down a tree, I would spend the first four hours
sharpening my ax."

Sharpen your ax.

DISCUSSION QUESTIONS

1. On a scale of 1–10, how seriously are you taking your educational opportunities, and how can you improve that?

2. How do you prepare for the different roles you will take in life?

3. What can you do to sharpen your ax in your spiritual life, and how much time are you spending on it?

BIBLE PASSAGES FOR ADDITIONAL STUDY

I Peter 3:15

Proverbs 6:6–8

FOLLOW T.R.'S ADVICE

"Sometimes we focus so much
on what we don't have
that we fail to see, appreciate,
and use what we do have!"
—Jeff Dixon

"Shamgar, the son of Anath,
which slew of the Philistines,
six hundred men with an ox goad . . ."
—Judges 3:31

Who's your favorite US president? We have had some very interesting characters serve as president. Many were war heroes. Some were related (John and John Quincy Adams, William Henry and Benjamin Harrison, George H. W. and George W. Bush). Andrew Jackson, "Old Hickory," is the most interesting to me. As a nine- or ten-year-old boy, he was taken prisoner during the Revolutionary War. He was so stubborn, he refused to polish an English general's boots. The enraged general slashed young Jackson's face with a saber. Jackson wore that scar the rest of his life. (He also deeply resented the British because his brother and his mother died of diseases in a prison camp. His mother was a nurse to the prisoners there.) He was a war hero. He was tough on Native Americans. He killed a man in Kentucky who said bad things about his beloved wife, Rachel. He lost an election even though he received the most popular votes. He finally became president and widely used the spoils system to reward his supporters.

Historians rank former presidents into categories and the following are my personal choices for these categories:

- **Great:** Washington, Lincoln, F. Roosevelt
- **Near Great:** Teddy Roosevelt, Truman
- **Above Average:** Reagan, Coolidge
- **Average:** Clinton, Eisenhower
- **Below Average:** L. Johnson, A. Johnson
- **Poor:** Grant, Harding
- **Tragic:** Carter

(I'll never forgive Carter for giving away the Panama Canal. He's condemned to his own wretched category.)

Most historians would put Teddy Roosevelt in the "great" or "near great" category. He rebuilt the US Navy. He won the Nobel Peace Prize for helping to end the Russo-Japanese War. He set aside more US land for national parks than all the previous presidents combined.

Teddy Roosevelt also gave all of us great advice when he said, "Do what you can, with what you have, where you are." It doesn't matter if you are six years old like our granddaughter

Elena, in your eighties like my dad, or anywhere in between. This applies to everyone.

> **Do what you can,**
> **with what you have,**
> **where you are.**

Do: Get going. You've probably heard the old riddle about five frogs sitting on a log and four deciding to jump in the water. Now how many frogs are on the log? The answer is . . . five. There is a difference between deciding to jump in and actually following through and jumping in. What you intend to do doesn't count. What you are going to do—really soon— doesn't matter. Nike tells us to get busy: *Just do it.*

What You Can: God has given each of us abilities to use for His work and His glory. Some can play ball. Others have amazing artistic ability. Some have musical talent. Others are good at math or science. Some are great encouragers. Figure out what gifts you have been given. Use those gifts. Do what you can.

With What You Have: A common mistake many people make is they don't do what they can because they worry about what they don't have. I can't sing. I can't play an instrument. I'm not good at math, science, English, or geography. I don't speak a foreign language (other than the word *fajitas* or other menu options at El Metate). I've never written a play or a movie. I've never been fast. (My college baseball coach once said if I got in a footrace with a pregnant woman that I'd finish a distant third. I resented that. I never denied it, but I still resented it.)

Stop comparing yourself to others. It's foolish to worry about what you can't do. Worrying about what you don't have is a waste of time. Get busy. Get busy doing what you can with what you have. Don't think, *When I'm an upperclassman I will volunteer* or *When I'm in college I'll go on a mission trip.* Do it now!

- Help today.
- Serve today.
- Volunteer today.
- Pray for someone today.
- Give today.
- Sacrifice today.
- Encourage today.
- Be a blessing today.

Where You Are: Today. It's not what you are going to do when you graduate, or when you get married, or when you get your truck paid off, or when the kids are grown, or when the Cubs win the World Series. Today!

The person I think who best exemplified Teddy Roosevelt's advice is an Old Testament character. He is found in Judges 3. He is only found in two verses of scripture, and one of them is the so-and-so begat him and he begat Sam and Sam begat, etc. His name is Shamgar.

In the last verse of Judges 3, we are told that Shamgar killed six hundred Philistines with an ox goad. It was wartime. The Philistines had invaded. Shamgar wanted to protect his family. But what could Shamgar do?

He was just one guy. He wasn't big and strong like Samson, who killed thousands of Philistines. He didn't have a BA from Cal Poly and a master's from MIT He was probably not well educated. He didn't have books and a laptop in his hand. He had a stick. An ox goad was a stick used to poke the ox to get it to plow if it stopped or got distracted. He was probably a farmer. He wasn't a SEAL or a ninja.

- Don't worry about what you can't do.
- Don't worry about what you don't have.
- Don't compare yourself to anyone else.

Hey, Samson killed a one-thousand-man army by himself with the jawbone of a donkey. Whatever little contribution Shamgar could make would pale in comparison to mighty Samson. But he did what he could with what he had. It makes me want to stand on a chair and applaud!

I'll be honest. If I lived in Old Testament times and the last verse of Judges 3 told my story, it would read something like this: "Then Coach T. sat around and talked about how many Philistines he would have killed if he had a submachine gun or an M1 tank." Shamgar didn't compare his bicep to Samson's. He didn't worry about what he didn't have. He just got busy.

With all due respect to Teddy Roosevelt, let's add one more thing: **prayer**. When God blesses our efforts, we get what He can do. Without prayer, we only get what a human can do. Have you ever noticed how some people are very talented musicians, but their music is just okay? Others have that special anointing by God that just stirs folks' souls. Hey, that's what Shamgar had. He had the blessing of God on his life.

I need God's anointing when I teach. I can give information, but God can bring about a transformation when He shows up. This is why prayer is vital for a successful teacher.

We don't know how he killed those six hundred soldiers with a stick. The Bible doesn't tell us. I suspect he got 'em one or two at a time. What I do know is this:

> He did what he could,
> with what he had,
> where he was
> after he prayed about it.

Our little granddaughters who are in the first and third grades do what they can to help their moms take care of the younger ones. Their great-grandpa teaches a Bible class on Monday nights. They follow Shamgar's example. Let's do the same. Let's follow Teddy Roosevelt's advice. It doesn't matter if you are five or eighty-five or anywhere in between: get busy!

DISCUSSION QUESTIONS

1. What can you do to influence others today?

2. What gifts have you been given to serve others?

3. How does your prayer life affect your ability to serve others?

BIBLE PASSAGE FOR ADDITIONAL STUDY

Judges 3:31

LIFE LESSON 28

ALWAYS UP OR GETTING UP

"Toughness is not the ability to persist
but the ability to start over."
—F. Scott Fitzgerald

"And let us not be weary in well doing:
for in due season we shall reap,
if we faint not."
—Galatians 6:9

Everybody makes mistakes. Nobody is perfect. We all
stumble. We all get knocked down. The real test of our
character is what we do when we get knocked down.

- Do we quit?
- Do we blame others?
- Do we make an excuse?
- Do we scramble to our feet and get back in the battle?

On February 19, 1962, Muhammad Ali fought Sonny
Banks at Madison Square Garden in New York City. Ali

was a heavy 5-1 favorite against the twenty-one-year-old unknown from Detroit. A small crowd of around two thousand was stunned when Banks dropped Ali to the canvas with a lightning-fast left hook in the first round. It was the first time in Ali's professional career that he had been knocked down. Ali was probably more embarrassed and surprised than hurt by the punch.

Ali scrambled to his feet with newly found resolve. The second round was a round in which Ali fired a stream of left-right combination punches. Most of Ali's missiles were directed at Banks's head. Late in the second round, Ali dropped Banks on the seat of his pants with a wicked left hook of his own. Banks was hurt but got through the round.

The third round was more of the same. Ali's blistering attack punished Banks relentlessly. Twice, Banks had to grab hold of the ropes to stay on his feet. Dr. Alexander Schiff took a look at Banks after the third round. He told the referee to keep a close eye on the beleaguered fighter. With twenty-six seconds left in the fourth round, referee Ruby Goldstein stopped the fight. Banks was unable to defend himself.

After the fight, a reporter asked Ali what he was thinking when he got knocked down in the first round. He said he thought *This [the canvas] is no place for a champion.* Ali was the greatest fighter of all time (the GOAT). *The greatest of all time* and he got knocked down. And more important, he got back up.

Everybody gets knocked down. It could be financially, socially, physically, spiritually, or emotionally. We get knocked down in different ways, but we all get knocked down. Pat

Summit, Coach K., Peyton Manning, Nick Saban, and Lebron James have all won a lot of games and championships. But they don't win every time.

The next time you get knocked down, remember: It's not the knockdown that matters. It's the get-up. Everybody gets knocked down. The canvas is no place for a champion. My coaching buddy, Chris Randall, says, "We are always up, or we're getting up." I like that.

> **Everybody gets knocked down, but if we respond correctly we'll be remembered for the get-up rather than the knockdown.**

DISCUSSION QUESTIONS

1. What are some things that can knock you down and make it hard to get back up?

2. Tell us about a time you were knocked down.

3. Why would anyone ever think quitting is the answer?

4. How does quitting set a bad precedent for the future?

BIBLE PASSAGE FOR ADDITIONAL STUDY

James 1:2–4

COWBOY UP

"Toughness is in the soul, not in the muscles."
—Alex Karras

"For the good that I would I do not:
but the evil which I would not, that I do."
—Romans 7:19

W hen our granddaughter Alivia was three years old, she spent the night with Vicky and me. Josh and Abbie went to Atlanta for the night and we were excited to have her for the evening. We all had a great time and went to bed.

Around 4:30 a.m., my wife got a phone call from her work. Vicky is a neonatal intensive care unit nurse. It had snowed a couple of inches that night. A few inches of snow is no big deal in Ohio, where I am from originally. Ohio is flat. Snow in Tennessee is a *huge* deal. We have mountains in Tennessee. We rarely have snow. We don't salt or plow the roads. We just wait until it melts. Even on the few times it does snow where we live, it rarely lasts longer than two or three hours.

The unit called Vicky because they had an urgent need for her to come in and work. Many of their nurses live on mountains that surround Chattanooga. Since it snows much more at higher elevations, and since you cannot risk driving down steep mountains after a recent snow, the hospital would be short-handed. Vicky agreed to go in because she would be able to get into work without jeopardizing her safety. She is a team player.

She woke me up and told me the situation. I was a little concerned about taking care of Alivia, but Vicky assured me I could handle a three-year-old for five or six hours until her parents came back. ("Alivia will sleep until nine anyway." "You raised three kids." "We have Cinnamon Toast Crunch . . .")

Alivia did sleep until about nine a.m. She watched cartoons until she was hungry enough for some cereal. After breakfast, she wanted to dress herself. I handed over her bag and told her I could help if she needed it. From the other room she hollered, "Big Daddy, do I put on a Pull-Up, or do I put my big girl pants on?"

You know what Pull-Ups are, right? They are disposable training pants for kids. She was pretty well potty-trained but used a Pull-Up at night just in case she had an accident. She never used one during the daytime. I told her to put her big girl pants on. "Be sure to tell Big Daddy if you need to go to the bathroom. I will help you. But we don't wear Pull-Ups during the day. Put on your big girl pants."

Life lesson number twenty-nine is *cowboy/cowgirl up*. There is a time and a place for Pull-Ups. There comes a time to put your big boy pants on. When young children are being potty-trained, they sometimes get distracted while playing with a new toy. They might have an accident. We understand—they're children. But we don't make excuses for them when they are six or seven and in school all day. It's time to grow up and take responsibility for themselves.

There is a point where you have to cowboy up. You have to be mature when things don't go your way. You have to study when you'd rather hang out with friends. You have to go to work even though you have the sniffles and feel tired. You have to go to school, even though it is raining and you are tired from staying up late watching *Sunday Night Football* (because the Broncos were on). And it's Monday. You have to go to the dentist. You have to pay your taxes. You can't say, "I don't feel like it."

One of the best examples I can give you to illustrate this principle is very personal. I am a diabetic. It's a complex disease that presents a lot of problems. For me to deal with diabetes, I have to manage my stress level, exercise, watch what I eat, and take all my medicines. I take four different types of meds every day. I have to give myself three shots every day. I take a shot of Byetta about an hour before I eat lunch and another an hour before I eat supper (dinner for some folks). I also take a shot of Lantus right before going to bed. *That's three shots every day!* If I don't give myself those injections every day, my blood sugar gets too high. The elevated blood sugar level results in me feeling sluggish physically and dazed mentally. It's kind of like walking around in a fog. I struggle to find the word I want to use. My speech becomes slurred and I can't process information as well as usual. All of these problems make it difficult for a guy who communicates for a living.

Do you think I look forward to taking those shots every day? Absolutely not! I despise it. I dread it. But sometimes you have to do what you don't want to do. You gotta cowboy up! Mature people understand they sometimes have to do things that are unpleasant. That's life. I must take those shots or there are serious consequences.

Think about your own life. Are there things that you need to do to improve your future? Maybe you need to remove some friends from your life because they influence you in negative ways. Maybe you like to spend money rather than save for college or retirement. Maybe you have a hard time respecting your parents or your boss because of generational disagreements. ("'Because I said so' is not really a good reason.") Maybe you need to cut up your credit cards. Maybe the person you're dating is not helping you to walk closer to the Lord and you need to break up with him or her. Maybe you have a toxic attitude that you know you have to change, but you tell yourself and others that you are a "realist."

Look yourself in the mirror. Be unwaveringly honest. Sometimes you need to do things you don't want to do.

Cowboy up!

DISCUSSION QUESTIONS

1. What are you hoping someone else will do for you that you should do for yourself?

2. Why do mature people do the hard things without complaining?

3. Does complaining about hard circumstances/tasks ever give any benefits?

BIBLE PASSAGES FOR ADDITIONAL STUDY

Isaiah 41:31

Joshua 1:9

LIFE LESSON 30

LIFE'S NOT FAIR

"My life has a superb cast
but I can't figure out the plot."
—Ashleigh Brilliant

"Life is what we make it,
always has been, always will be."
—Grandma Moses

A recent movement in the United States is a group of people complaining about the top 1 percent of Americans making too much money. They call themselves the Occupy Movement and they are protesting. They are holding sit-ins and camping out at public places. The protesters occupied Wall Street in NYC and pitched tents on the lawn at the courthouse in Chattanooga. Do you think some people make too much money? Is it unfair for a few to make millions (or even billions) when others struggle just to have basic food, clothing, and shelter?

In Psalm 73, David asked, "Why do the wicked prosper and the righteous suffer?" Best-selling author Scott Peck began his book *The Road Less Traveled* saying, "Life is difficult." It sounds like not much has changed in 2,500 years, doesn't it?

I agree with Steve Mariboli when he says, "The only thing that makes life unfair is the delusion that it should be fair." Life can be a struggle with runaway inflation, high health care costs, unemployment, and rising crime rates. Some companies are downsizing. The stock market resembles a roller coaster. While we tend to think of the many challenges facing Americans today, what if we lived in Rwanda or Bosnia? I'd say our definition of adversity would be much different if we lived in those war-torn countries.

> **Don't expect life to be fair. Look at life as opportunities.**
> **Life can be challenging; let's accept the challenge. Let's meet it head-on.**

Life can be beautiful. Holding a newborn baby or watching a toddler stagger a few steps can bring a smile to your face. Seeing the majesty of the Grand Canyon or the Andes Mountains in South America will make you shake your head in amazement. A week of vacation at the beach in Destin with emerald-green water and snow-white sand is so relaxing. A late afternoon hot-air balloon ride in Albuquerque into a New Mexico sunset can take your breath away.

Maybe C. J. Redwine said it best in her book *Defiance*: "It's probably my job to tell you life isn't fair, but I figure you already know that. So instead, I'll tell you that hope is precious, and you're right not to give up."

The good guy doesn't always get the girl. Your team won't win every game. Criminals will get away with it sometimes. The referee will miss some calls. The boss won't see all the extra work that you did while two coworkers slipped out early. Good people get sick and die at a young age. That's life. Let's step up to the plate and take our cuts. Life will throw us some nasty curve balls, but we'll take the challenge.

Life's not fair.

DISCUSSION QUESTIONS

1. Why do bad things sometimes happen to good people?

2. Why doesn't the good guy always get the girl?

3. Is life harder for some people than it is for others?

BIBLE PASSAGE FOR ADDITIONAL STUDY

Matthew 20:1–16

LIFE LESSON 31

SEMPER GUMBY

"Be clear about your goal
but flexible about the process of achieving it."
—Brian Tracy

"Stay committed to your decisions
but stay flexible in your approach."
—Tom Robbins

When I was very small, I used to watch a strange little guy named Gumby and his friend Pokey. Pokey was a horse. Gumby had a really unusually shaped head and unusually shaped feet. He kind of shuffled when he walked. I watched Gumby and Pokey on an old black-and-white television.

At age eight or nine, I was given Gumby and Pokey toys to play with. I learned that Gumby was green and Pokey was orange. I loved those toys. The toys were soft rubber that had been molded around tiny flexible wires. You could twist Gumby's arms to signal a touchdown or twist his feet (he didn't have toes). His feet could touch his ears or cross behind his head. I spent a lot of hours playing with those toys. The only real limits on the contortions they could do were the limits of your imagination.

If you stopped playing with them for the day, Gumby and Pokey stayed right where you put them. They were frozen in place until you decided to have one stand on his head or hug a pencil or whatever.

We could all learn something from these toys. They were always adaptable to any situation they were placed in. So I say we all need to follow the motto "Semper Gumby."

"Semper Gumby" means "always flexible." It means we don't get easily upset when things don't go the way we thought they would. We understand that circumstances change. We can adapt to unexpected disappointments. If things get off schedule we can improvise. We don't worry about whose fault it is or why it happened to us. We don't get flustered or angry.

Boxers call this "rolling with the punches." They lean away from a punch to lessen its impact. It's a lot smarter to do that than to stubbornly stand your ground and refuse to avoid the full impact of a punch.

Are you easily upset when something throws off your schedule? Do you get angry and "blow up" when things go wrong? Do you worry more about fixing blame than fixing a problem? How do you respond when someone is five minutes late? How about if they tell you they will do something, but they only complete half of the job?

Let's be clear. I am not talking about being a sellout to something that is crucial. There are some people I would die for. There are some things that I believe I would give my life for. These are things I can't compromise under any circumstances. We are not talking about weakness or giving in to something that is wrong.

In 1997 Richard Carlson wrote a book of essays that were designed to help prevent the little annoyances in life from driving you over a cliff. The name of his book said it best: *Don't Sweat the Small Stuff . . . and It's All Small Stuff.* Basically, Carlson was saying, "Chill out. It's not that big of a deal. Things will work out. There's no need to panic."

This lesson will be more difficult for some folks who just love structure and a schedule. Others will be less challenged to apply the Semper Gumby approach to their lives.

The next time you sense you are going on tilt over some tiny issue, just let it go. Semper Gumby, always flexible, is a better way to live than getting angry and calling your lawyer every time the neighbor kid's ball rolls into your yard.

"Be firm on principle but flexible on method." —Zig Ziglar

DISCUSSION QUESTIONS

1. Why do we need to be flexible?

2. Why is it hard to be flexible?

3. If we are flexible, won't people take advantage of us?

BIBLE PASSAGE FOR ADDITIONAL STUDY

Colossians 3:1–25

GET OUT OF TOWN

"It isn't what you have that makes
you happy or unhappy.
It is what you think about it."
—Dale Carnegie

"And having food and raiment
let us be therewith content."
—I Timothy 6:8

In Genesis 12:11, God tells Abraham to leave his home and family to go elsewhere. He was from Ur-Kasdim, which in English is Ur of the Chaldees. In 1927 an archeologist named Leonard Woolley identified Ur's location as a city in the southern part of Mesopotamia. It was a sacred city of the moon god Nanna, full of temples and groves where the Sumerians worshipped.

We don't live in Mesopotamia. You probably haven't been invited to worship the moon recently. (And if you were asked to do that, you'd probably have a tough time not laughing in the face of the person who asked you.)

Many people worldwide still live in ER. That's E-R, not UR. I'd say the vast majority of Americans live in ER. They obsess about figuring out a way to be:

taller	happier	skinnier
richer	smarter	younger
wittier	healthier	prettier
	stronger	

When it comes to their house, they'd like something:

newer	closer	better
nicer	bigger	fancier

Or they are not satisfied with their car unless it's:

faster	newer	fancier
cooler	nicer	bigger

The same thing applies to our job or career. Even if we like our job, we want something higher.

We are never satisfied. The problem is when we get what we want, we want something else. Something more. We want to be the:

tallest	happiest	skinniest
richest	smartest	youngest
wittiest	healthiest	prettiest
	strongest	

If our house is newer, that makes us satisfied until we see one that is the newest, the nicest, the biggest, and the best. The new-car smell hasn't even worn off, but we are envious because someone else's ride is the fastest, coolest, newest, fanciest, or whatever. We just have a tough time being content.

If you have traveled overseas, you realize how blessed we are to live here in the United States. I have visited countries where people work very hard and earn $250 in a year. Only 7 percent of the world's population owns any kind of a car. Yet we complain if the air-conditioning in our car isn't stellar.

Here's what I know after coaching for thirty-five years: you can never win enough. If you win twenty basketball games and win the regular-season district title, you are not satisfied. You feel you must win the district tournament. If you win the district tourney, you want to win the region. Won the region title? So what? You gotta win that sub-state game. So you win the sub-state and make it to the big show. Are you satisfied? No way. You want to win it all. If you win it all, you need to repeat to prove it wasn't a fluke. You can never win enough.

John Wooden was known as the Wizard of Westwood. He coached the UCLA Bruins to ten national championships in a twelve-year period. Ten! UCLA won eighty-eight games in a row at one point. From the 1966–1967 season through the 1972–1973 campaign, the Bruins captured seven NCAA titles in a row. Needless to say, getting to the Final Four is a tremendous feat. Many great coaches never get their teams to one Final Four. Remember: the NCAA tournament is not double elimination. If you lose once during the tournament, you go home. So many bad things can cost you: an illness of a star player, a bad call by an official, a hot shooting opponent, a sprained ankle, an "off night" by key players, or maybe a mistake by the coach.

Wooden's teams won seven in a row. In the 1974 NCAA tournament, UCLA was beaten by North Carolina State in the Final Four. The following year, UCLA beat Memphis to reclaim the crown. It was their eighth in nine years!

As Wooden exited the floor, a wealthy UCLA alum excitedly said, "You let us down last year, Coach, but we got 'em this year!" Wooden never coached again. He coached two years at Indiana State and twenty-seven years at UCLA. Wooden's teams won ten titles, the same as Dean Smith, Roy Williams, Bob Knight, and Mike Krzyzewski combined. Yet to some it wasn't enough.

Oil tycoon J. Paul Getty was the richest man in the United States in 1957. He was a billionaire. He was also a miser who had a pay phone installed in the lobby of his home. On July 10, 1973, Getty's sixteen-year-old grandson, JPG III, was kidnapped. The elder Getty refused to pay the ransom. In November a newspaper received a box containing a lock of hair and JPG III's ear. They demanded $3 million within ten days or Getty would get his grandson back in little pieces.

Getty agreed to pay no more than $2.2 million, because that was the most he could deduct off his taxes. After his son begged him, Getty agreed to loan his son $800,000 at 4 percent interest to get his boy back. His son paid the ransom (with the help of that loan) and JPG III was released in southern Italy. After Getty III's release, he called to thank his grandfather, but the elder Getty refused to come to the phone. He was too busy.

John Paul Getty III was permanently traumatized and became addicted to painkilling drugs. At age twenty-four, he mixed drugs and alcohol, which led to a stroke. The stroke brought on paralysis, which lasted until he died at age fifty-four.

John Paul Getty left behind $2.7 billion when he died. (Remember, a billion is a thousand million. So 2,700 million wasn't enough for him to be willing to pay a ransom for a grandchild? *Wow!* Greedy much?)

We need to learn to be content. This is not something that we are naturally born with. We all have to learn to be content. Even the Apostle Paul said he was not easily satisfied in his life.

> "For I have learned, in whatsoever state I am, therewith to be content." —Philippians 4:11

If the Apostle Paul had to learn and relearn this lesson, it is understandable why we struggle to be satisfied with what we have.

God wanted Abraham to get out of Ur. He wants us to get out of ER. He wants us to be thankful. He wants us to be content with all He has given us. And never, ever forget this: we have so much to be thankful for!

DISCUSSION QUESTIONS

1. Why is it nearly impossible to be satisfied with what we have?

2. Why do we think material things, power, or fame will satisfy us?

3. What should make us satisfied?

4. Tell us about something you got that you thought would satisfy you (but it didn't).

BIBLE PASSAGE FOR ADDITIONAL STUDY

Philippians 4:11–13

THE LAST DUCK

"There is a lot of difference between
listening and hearing."
—G. K. Chesterton

"Hear counsel, and receive instruction,
that thou mayest be wise in thy latter end."
—Proverbs 19:20

I played some golf with some buddies of mine and had a great time. It was in August just as school was getting started. When I got home, I was delighted to see two of my favorite people in the world, my wife, Vicky, and our then-four-year-old granddaughter Alivia. They were in the swing on our back deck, singing, laughing, and reading books. We really enjoyed Alivia that evening. She beat me in Candyland (although it was very close). She reminded me that you have to be a good sport when you lose. It was really funny.

After Nana gave her a bath, Alivia told me that her mom and dad went to Atlanta on a date. She asked me what a date was. I told her a date was when you go out and spend time with someone who is special to you. Since her dad really loved her mom, he wanted to spend some time with her, just the two of them. They would go to Atlanta to a concert on Friday night. They would go to the Korean restaurant the next day and be together until Sunday afternoon when they would come to pick her up at our house. Alivia said, "Do my mom and dad still love me, too?" I assured her that her parents would always love her, but Nana, Uncle Mitch, and Big Daddy were really excited to get to spend some time with her for a couple of days. Her mom and dad were nice enough to share her with us for a little while. This made us all very happy.

I asked Alivia if she would like to go on a date with me on Saturday morning. She wanted to know what we would do. I told her we would go to a playground and then the duck pond to feed the fish and ducks. We would go to McDonald's or Burger King, whoever had the best toy with their kids' meal. We were going to have fun. She got excited about our date. I was fired up about it as well.

I always enjoy Saturday mornings. Saturday is the one day of the week we get to sleep in. Our school starts at 7:15 a.m. You have to get up at oh-dark-hundred to get to school by seven. On Sundays, I teach an adult Sunday school class, so I get up early every Sunday as well. Saturday mornings are special.

At 6:45 a.m. the door to our room swung open. I could hear Alivia calling, "Big Daddy. Big Daddy. Big Daddy, wake up. It's time to go." I ignored her and hoped she would go away. No such luck. She slapped my face with her little hand. It stung pretty good. She was ready to go and would not be delayed. I got up and we ate some cereal. We popped two bags of popcorn in the microwave, strapped her in the car seat, and took off. We were both full of anticipation, and it would be a wonderful day.

We went to the playground first. Alivia headed for the swings. She loved to go higher and higher. She climbed the rock wall and slid down the slide. She rode the zip line. After some more swinging, we headed to the duck pond in East Lake.

She fed the fish, and the ducks hustled over to get their share. She loved it. There was one duck that got distracted by a barking beagle. Unfortunately for him, he was at the far side of the lake. By the time he realized that all the other ducks were enjoying a feast with our granddaughter, it was too late. Popcorn was being broadcasted in every direction, but he would get none. He really wanted to join in the fun. He desperately wanted to get fed. But there was no popcorn left by the time he arrived. It was all gone. The opportunity was lost.

Alivia was a little upset. She felt bad for the last duck. He was just too late and had missed his chance. Life lesson number thirty-three is *don't be the last duck.* No matter how upset you get, no matter how bad you want some popcorn, no matter how hungry you are, if you show up late you get left out. It's just that simple.

So how do you keep from being the last duck? You pay attention. You get to class on time. You don't miss meetings. You listen to your teachers and your parents. When you give attention to the details, you will not be the last duck. And you won't miss out on things that are a lot more meaningful than a bag of popcorn.

Good things happen when you are not the last duck.

DISCUSSION QUESTIONS

1. Tell us about something you missed out on because you didn't listen closely.

2. What are some benefits you get from being the first to arrive at a meeting, class, or concert?

BIBLE PASSAGES FOR ADDITIONAL STUDY

Proverbs 12:15
Proverbs 19:27

LIFE LESSON 34

KNOWING IS NOT ENOUGH

"When all is said and done, more is said than done."
—Aesop, 600 BC

"For if any be a hearer of the word,
and not a doer,
he is like unto a man beholding
his natural face in a glass:
For he beholdeth himself, and goeth
his way, and straightway forgetteth
what manner of man he was.
But whoso looketh into the perfect law
of liberty, and continueth therein,
he being not a forgetful hearer,
but a doer of the work,
this man shall be blessed in his deed."
—James 1:23–25

Knowledge is very important. I've been an educator all of my adult life. I realize how difficult the teaching profession is. As a matter of fact, I think teaching is a calling. I'm so thankful for the many amazing teachers I had who truly cared and patiently taught me along the way. My parents, Guy and Carol Templeton, would be at the top of that list.

> **Knowing is important, but doing is crucial.**

I can know that exercise is important for my future health and vitality, but do I get on that treadmill? You can be fully aware that watching your weight matters, but do you have that extra piece of cake (with ice cream on it)? Knowing you need to get your brakes fixed or your bald tires replaced will not prevent you from getting in a wreck. You must act on that knowledge.

You have probably heard it's dangerous to text and drive. If you are driving 60 miles per hour in your car, you will travel more than four hundred feet in the time it takes to glance down at a text. Four hundred feet is further than a football field from end zone to end zone. You know you shouldn't drive distracted, but do you answer texts while behind the wheel?

Nearly twenty-five years ago I was coaching a JV game at Tennessee Temple Academy. (I coached the JV and the varsity at that time. It helped build continuity in the program. I was also much younger/more energetic/dumber than I am now.) During the second game of the year, one of our sophomore guards, Matt, saw a ball going out of bounds. He dove over the end line and slapped the ball back into play. He was really hustling, which was something we greatly valued in our program. Outworking our opponents was always a point of emphasis for our coaches and a sense of pride for our players.

Matt was a great kid. He was very smart. He was a hard worker. He was extremely coachable. A couple of years later, he played a big role in our district and region titles. But in this case, Matt's hustle worked against us. He saved the ball by batting it back inbounds to a player on the other team, *directly under their basket*. Our opponent calmly laid the ball in the basket. It was two points for the bad guys.

It was my fault. I had emphasized the hustle aspect of basketball, but I neglected to mention the "don't save the ball to just anybody who is standing under the other team's goal" principle. At halftime, I taught all the guys that if the ball is going out under the other team's basket, we have two options. First, grab the ball and heave it as far as you can toward our basket. We might not get it, but at worst our opponents won't get an easy basket. Our second option would be to just grab it and go ahead and step out of bounds. This strategy would prevent the opposition from saving it for an easy basket, and it would also allow us to set our defense. All the fellas understood.

As fate would have it, there was another loose ball under the opponent's basket in the fourth quarter. Matt saved the ball. *To our opponents! And they scored! Again!* I still remember Matt running back down the court pointing at himself. He was shaking his head. He knew he had misplayed that one.

I put in a sub for Matt. He felt bad. He never wanted to hurt the team. He said, "My bad, Coach. I know I shouldn't save the ball under their basket." I'm not sure exactly what I said, but I'm sure it was something along the lines of: "It's not enough to know what you're supposed to do. *Ya gotta do it!*"

I got a speeding ticket the other day. I knew the speed limit was 65. I drove much faster than that. The officer asked me if I knew what the speed limit was. I had no excuse. (I'm now hoping for a merciful judge.)

It's not enough to know that drugs are dangerous or that alcohol and tobacco can be addictive. Ask almost anyone who uses a tobacco product if they realize it is a dangerous product. They know it is dangerous. It's written right on the package. But too often, the nicotine wins.

You know you must manage the stress in your life better. You know exercise needs to be a daily habit. You know you need to pray more and worry less. You know you need to eat healthier foods. You know you need to buckle that seatbelt every time, obey the speed limit, and avoid driving while distracted by a cell phone. You know you should serve others more and be less selfish.

> **It's not what you know. What you
> do is what really matters.
> Be determined to follow through on
> the things you've been taught.**

DISCUSSION QUESTIONS

1. Why is it easier to teach a lesson than to do it?

2. Tell us about something you knew you should or shouldn't do but did not follow through on it.

3. Tell us about something you are going to do or not do, starting today.

BIBLE PASSAGE FOR ADDITIONAL STUDY

James 1:22

DON'T QUIT

"A hero is an ordinary individual
who finds the strength to persevere in spite
of overwhelming obstacles."
—Christopher Reeve

"Where the battle rages,
there the loyalty of the soldier is proven."
—Martin Luther

Have you ever started playing on a team and then quit before the season was over?

Did you ever start playing a musical instrument and then quit when the progress was too slow?

Anybody you know ever started a job and quit because it was much harder than they had anticipated?

Don't quit! You will fight the battle of wanting to quit throughout your life. Learn to win the battle now and you will be better off for it.

We moved to southern Ohio in the summer before I started the eighth grade. I met a guy about my age who was a very gifted musician. We became good friends. His name was Jim. He was a very good singer as well as an excellent trumpet player. I decided I would like to play the trumpet. It was much harder than I thought it would be, and I was much too lazy to put in the time necessary to learn the trumpet. I did not like the teacher and I dreaded the lessons. (Of course, I would not have dreaded the lessons if I had practiced like I should have.) The progress was slow, so I simply stopped going to the lessons. I still regret not following through on the trumpet.

Paul W. "Bear" Bryant was a legendary college football coach. He was the head coach at four Division I universities. He retired as the winningest coach in college football history with 323 career victories. He was inducted into the College Football Hall of Fame in 1986. During a twenty-five year tenure at the University of Alabama, Coach Bryant's teams won six national championships and thirteen conference championships. If there was one thing Coach Bryant's teams would be known for, it would be resiliency. No Alabama team would ever be accused of quitting. Regardless of the circumstance, the Crimson Tide would never let down or give up. His teams were always tough.

Coach Bryant always taught his players that the first time you quit it would be difficult. You'd feel bad about it. You would have regrets. The second time you quit, it would be much easier. And the third time, he said, you wouldn't even think about it at all. It would just be a habit. Quitting would become very easy. This is why the coach always emphasized to his players never to give up. He knew it would become a habit that would make it easier to give up when difficulties would arise on the football field or later on in life.

When your classes are hard, or your teachers are difficult to follow, don't quit. Don't look for the easy way out. You have to keep going. When your parents misunderstand you, you have to press on. You can't have a pity party for yourself. When you have difficulties on the job, you have to work things out. When the car won't start, the refrigerator is broken, and the baby is sick, you can't just quit. When your kids disappoint you for the third week in a row, you don't give up on them. If there are problems in your marriage, the answer is love and patience and communication, not abandoning the ship. If the doctor tells you that the test results are back and the prognosis is grim, what will your response be?

Hopefully, your response will be to fight back. Keep the faith. Get an aggressive treatment plan and stick with it. It will be much easier to have that type of reaction if you have been resilient in the face of adversity. If your habit has been to quit, it is doubtful that you will have the resolve necessary to fight back against any hardships that you face throughout life.

Rick Warren says you have three choices when bad things happen.

1. You can let it destroy you. (Boo hoo! I lost the match.)
2. You can let it define you. (I am a loser. I might as well get *loser* tattooed on my forehead.)
3. You can let it develop you. (What can I learn from this? How can I do better next time?)

If you let it define you, your mental image of yourself is that of a loser. Again, we are back to attitude.

> "Your life is your garden. Your thoughts are your seeds. If your life isn't awesome, you've been watering the weeds." —Nathan Poshwar

Since life is challenging and we may all be tempted to give up many times in the future, let's just decide today that we are not going to take the easy way out. When facing problems, we will look for solutions. When having relationship problems, we will communicate and seek to understand as well as to be understood. We will never give up on our families. If the economy turns bad, we will stay in there and dig a little deeper and work a little harder. What we will not do is give up. Quitting is just a bad habit that we never want to develop. Winston Churchill said, "Kites rise highest against the wind, not with it."

> **Don't quit!**

DISCUSSION QUESTIONS

1. What are reasons why weak people quit?

2. What are reasons why good people quit?

3. Who do you admire for never quitting even though they could have easily quit?

BIBLE PASSAGE FOR ADDITIONAL STUDY

Numbers 14:36–38

DON'T SELL
YOURSELF SHORT

"Nothing splendid has ever been achieved
except by those who dared believe
that something inside of them
was superior to circumstances."
—Bruce Barton

"I can do all things through
Christ which strengtheneth me."
—Philippians 4:13

On March 24, 1975, an obscure boxer named Chuck Wepner fought Muhammad Ali in a bout in Cleveland, Ohio. Ali was the heavyweight champion. Wepner was a bar bouncer who picked up fights when given the opportunity. Wepner was thought to be an easy knockout for Ali. Top fighters often inflate their records with fights against inferior opponents. Gaudy win-loss records with high knockout totals excite the fans. Fight promoters can sell more tickets to see a rising star with twenty wins and eighteen knockouts. The fans have no idea how good their competition is.

For a journeyman fighter, a fight against a big-name opponent offers visibility, a good payday, and an opportunity for glory. Maybe, just maybe, they can land their best shot and "be somebody." (So you're saying there's a chance.)

In truth, the chances of victory for an outclassed fighter are microscopic. He will be a light workout for a younger, faster, stronger fighter. If he had a legitimate chance to win, he wouldn't have been chosen for the bout. Often a fighter is selected because his skills have diminished. A fighter who is past his prime is in big trouble against the speed and power of a top contender.

Chuck Wepner fought fifty-one professional fights. He won thirty-five (seventeen by knockout) and lost fourteen. Two of Wepner's fights ended in a draw. His style was that he had no style; he was a brawler. He was easy to hit and he could take a punch.

Wepner fought some big-name fighters. He was knocked out in three rounds by George Foreman and Joe Bugner. He was knocked out in ten rounds by Sonny Liston. After the Liston fight, Wepner received seventy-two stitches in his face. He was thereafter known as the Bayonne Bleeder instead of the Bayonne Brawler.

Ali would receive $1.5 million for his title defense. Wepner got $100,000 for his biggest purse ever by far. Wepner trained hard for the fight. It was the first time he had trained full-time for a fight. Wepner told reporters, "I've been a survivor all my life. If I survived the marines, I can survive Ali." Wepner had won eleven of twelve fights before taking on Ali.

In the ninth round, Wepner knocked Ali down. (Ali later claimed Wepner stepped on his foot.) Ali knocked Wepner down on three occasions. Ali dominated Wepner in the later rounds. Wepner's eyes were both swollen and cut. His nose was broken. Though far behind on the scorecards, Wepner kept fighting. Ali knocked Wepner down with nineteen seconds left in the fifteenth round. He rose to his feet as the referee's count reached nine. Unwilling to see Wepner take any more punishment, the referee stopped the fight. Ali won by technical knockout.

Three time zones away, an out-of-work actor watched the fight on closed-circuit television in California. He was so inspired by Wepner's performance that he wrote for three days. It took him twenty hours to write the script. The actor was Sylvester Stallone. The screenplay was *Rocky*.

Stallone was turned down by several studios on his project. Finally, he was offered $400,000 for his screenplay. He was a starving actor and he turned down $400K! That would be about $900,000 today. Stallone's counteroffer to United Artists was:

1) Stallone would play the lead character for the minimum fee allowed.

2) Stallone would receive 1 percent of the gross profits.

The studio explained that if they never made the film or if it never made a profit, Stallone would get nothing. Stallone believed in himself and in his script.

Rocky was completed in twenty-eight days. (Stallone made $1,260 for the role—$340 a week.) The movie cost $1 million to make and $4 million to promote worldwide. It was the top film of 1976 and earned $225 million. *Rocky* received ten Academy Award nominations and it won three Oscars, including Best Picture.

Stallone wrote two of the biggest movie franchises in the six *Rocky* movies and four *Rambo* movies. He became one of Hollywood's highest-paid stars. His movies have generated $4 billion for the studios. Sylvester Stallone had gone from an unknown to being a huge star. He now has a net worth of around $400 million.

The point of this story is simple: never sell yourself short. What if Sylvester Stallone had sold his screenplay for $60,000? What if he didn't hold out for the chance to play the leading role? The 1 percent he got for the original *Rocky* probably resulted in him getting around $8 million in 1976. You can be sure he got a much higher percentage for the rest of those films. The Rocky and Rambo movies sold more than $2 billion in tickets. You also have shirts, action figures, toys, etc.

> **Don't settle. You can accomplish great things if you don't sell yourself short.**

The rest of the story is this: United Artists wanted Chuck Wepner as a technical advisor for the first *Rocky*. They wanted to learn more about how he trained so they could flesh out the story. United Artists offered Wepner roughly the same deal they offered Stallone: $70,000 or 1 percent of the net profit. Chuck thought he was taking the "sure thing." He cost himself approximately $8 million.

Chuck Wepner is now seventy-four years old. He works at a liquor store called Majestic Wines and Spirits in Carlstadt,

> *Don't sell yourself short!*
> **You have the ability.**
> **Do you have the courage *to go for***
> ***it* and make things happen?**
> ***Dream big dreams.***
> **Do something *great* with the gifts *God* has given you!**

New Jersey (eight miles northwest of New York City).

Never underestimate what you can accomplish through hard work, faith, and the favor of God.

Live your life to the hilt!

DISCUSSION QUESTIONS

1. Why do we settle for less than we could achieve?

2. Who do you know who had a big dream and went for it?

3. What goal would you like to accomplish?

4. What are you going to do this week to achieve your goal?

BIBLE PASSAGE FOR ADDITIONAL STUDY

Philippians 4:6

SOURCES

Life Lesson 1: To the Hilt
1. Coxhead, Margaret Duncan, "Cortes 'Burns his Boats,'" in *Mexico* (London: T. C. & E. C. Jack, 1909), 96-103.

Life Lesson 3: What Kind of Soldier Are You?
1. "Ronald Reagan - First Inaugural Address," Reagan 2020, accessed August 1, 2014, http://reagan2020.us/speeches/First_Inaugural.asp.

2. Halloran, Richard, "The Pledge of Private Treptow," *New York Times*, January 21, 1981, http://www.nytimes.com/1981/01/21/us/the-pledge-of-private-treptow.html.

3. "General Gives His Stars to a Wounded Marine Washington," *New York Times*, November 16, 1983, http://www.nytimes.com/1983/11/16/world/general-gives-his-stars-wounded-marine-washington-nov-15-ap-marine-commandant.html.

4. "Marine Looks Back on Beirut Bombing," *New York Times*, December 2, 1986, http://www.nytimes.

com/1986/12/02/us/marine-looks-back-on-beirut-bombing.html.

5. Withrow, Steve. "Semper Fi in Beirut," Charactercin-cinnati.org, accessed August 1, 2014, http://www.charactercincinnati.org/Faith/Qualities/Dependability/-1-Min-Semper%20Fi%20in%20Beirut.doc.

Life Lesson 4: Choices and Consequences

1. "James Brooks," NFL.com, accessed March 28, 2014, http://www.nfl.com/player/jamesbrooks/2499809/profile.

2. "Cris Carter," NFL.com, accessed March 28, 2014, http://www.nfl.com/player/criscarter/2500011/profile.

3. Paschall, David, "Extent of Bowman's Fall 'Really Too Bad,'" *Times Free Press* (Chattanooga, TN), April 30, 2008.

Life Lesson 5: You Make Your Choices.

1. Stone, Michael, "Teen 'Starting All Over,'" *Times Free Press* (Chattanooga, TN), December 3, 2010, http://www.timesfreepress.com/news/2010/dec/03/teen-starting-all-over.

2. "Justin Verlander Stats," Baseball Almanac, accessed March 15, 2014, http://www.baseball-almanac.com/players/player.php?p=verlaju01.

3. Kapler, Gabe, "DUI Victim Tufano Hopes Matt Bush Can Right His Ways," FOX Sports, accessed March

16, 2014, http://www.foxsports.com/mlb/story/matt-bush-victim-anthony-tufano-speaks-out-about-recovery-from-motorcycle-accident-050514.

Life Lesson 6: If You Live for the Moment . . .
1. "Hornets' Phills, 30, Killed in Car Crash," ESPN.com, accessed March 20, 2014, http://assets.espn.go.com/nba/news/2000/0112/285010.html.

Life Lesson 7: Some Things You Can't Play With.
1. "Man Drowns in Orca Pool at SeaWorld Orlando," Environment News Service, July 7, 1999, http://www.ens-newswire.com/ens/jul1999/1999-07-07-01.asp.

Life Lesson 10: The Crucial Choice
1. Lucado, Max, "A Heart Like His," in *Just Like Jesus* (Nashville, TN: Word Pub., 1998), 4–5.

Life Lesson 14: Find Your Sweet Spot
1. Plumb, Charlie, "Parachute Packer Story," Captain Charlie Plumb, accessed August 28, 2013, http://speaker.charlieplumb.com/about-captain/parachute-story/.

2. Maxwell, John C., "The Law of the Niche," in *The 17 Indisputable Laws of Teamwork: Embrace Them and Empower Your Team* (Nashville, TN: Thomas Nelson, 2001), 37–39.

Life Lesson 20: Principles of Friendship IV
1. "Without Bias," *ESPN Films 30 for 30*, volume 1, episode 5 (March 11, 2009), DVD.

Life Lesson 21: Everyone Preaches Their Own Memorial
1. Covey, Stephen R., "Principles of Personal Leadership," in *The Seven Habits of Highly Effective People: Restoring the Character Ethic* (New York: Simon and Schuster, 1989), 96–97.

Life Lesson 22: It's Hard to Run a Race in a Raincoat
1. Coffee, Wayne, "Olympics 2012: Usain Bolt Wins His Third London Gold Medal, Anchors Jamaica to World Record in the 4x100 Relay," *New York Daily News*, August 11, 2012, http://www.nydailynews.com/sports/olympics-2012/olympics-2012-usain-bolt-wins-london-gold-medal-anchors-jamaica-world-record-4x100-relay-article-1.1134456.

Life Lesson 26: Can You Beat Me?
1. McNamara, Robert, "Abe Lincoln and His Axe: Reality Behind the Legend," About.com, accessed January 28, 2014, http://history1800s.about.com/od/abrahamlincoln/ss/Abe-Lincoln-and-His-Ax.htm.

2. White, Ronald C., "Persistent in Learning," in *A. Lincoln: A Biography* (New York: Random House, 2009), 36–41.

Life Lesson 27: Follow T.R.'s Advice
1. Morris, Edmund, "Moral Overstrain," in *Theodore Rex* (New York: Random House, 2002), 519.

2. "Quotations by Author: Theodore Roosevelt, 1858–1919," The Quotations Page, accessed August 2, 2014,

http://www.quotationspage.com/quotes/Theodore_
Roosevelt.

Life Lesson 28: Always Up or Getting Up

1. "It's Not About the Knockdown," Boxing Motivation,
   Ian Humphrey audiotape excerpt, https://www.you-
   tube.com/watch?v=drYvm0-c0Z0.

Life Lesson 30: Life's Not Fair

1. Maraboli, Steve, "Each Day Is a Lifetime," in *Unapolo-
   getically You: Reflections on Life and the Human Experience* (Port Washington, NY: A Better Today, 2013),
   105.

Life Lesson 32: Get Out of Town

1. Davis, Seth, "Farewell," in *Wooden: A Coach's Life*
   (New York: Times Books, 2014), 440, 526.

2. Gaston, Teddy Getty, and Digby Diehl, "Siena,"
   in *Alone Together: My Life with J. Paul Getty* (New
   York: Ecco/Harper Collins, 2013), 189–190.

3. Weber, Bruce, "J. Paul Getty III, 54, Dies; Had Ear
   Cut Off by Captors," *New York Times*, February 7,
   2011, http://www.nytimes.com/2011/02/08/world/
   europe/08gettyobit.html?_r=0.

Life Lesson 35: Don't Quit

1. Roberts, Drew, "Top 50 Quotes from Bear Bryant,"
   Saturday Down South, August 7, 2012, http://www.
   saturdaydownsouth.com/2012/bear-bryant-50-quotes.

2. "Football Coaches: Bear Bryant," Coaching Roots, accessed June 29, 2014, http://coachingroots.com/football/coaches/bear-bryant.

3. D'Avolio, Lauren, "Rick Warren on 'Surrender: The Path to Peace,'" *The Gospel Herald*, September 4, 2013, http://www.gospelherald.com/article/church/48782/rick-warren-on-surrender-the-path-to-peace.htm.

Life Lesson 36: Don't Sell Yourself Short

1. Raskin, Eric, "'Real Rocky' Wepner Finally Getting Due," ESPN.com, October 25, 2011, http://espn.go.com/boxing/story/_/page/IamChuckWepner/chuck-wepner-recognized-rocky-fame.

2. White, James, "The Story Behind Rocky," Total Film: The Modern Guide to Movies, October 26, 2009, http://www.totalfilm.com/features/the-story-behind-rocky.

3. "Ali-Wepner Fight," The Encyclopedia of Cleveland History, accessed April 20, 2014, http://www.ech.case.edu/cgi/article.pl?id=AF2.

4. "Chuck Wepner," BoxRec, accessed May 2, 2014, http://boxrec.com/list_bouts.php?human_id=97&cat=boxer.

5. Milani, Jerry, "35 Years After Facing Muhammad Ali, 'Bayonne Bleeder' Chuck Wepner Still Pulls No Punches," newjerseynewsroom.com, March 23, 2010, http://www.newjerseynewsroom.com/professional/35-

years-after-facing-muhammad-ali-bayonne-bleeder-
chuck-wepner-still-pulls-no-punches.

6. "Sylvester Stallone Net Worth," Celebrity Net Worth,
   accessed September 2, 2014, http://www.celebritynet-
   worth.com/richest-celebrities/actors/sylvester-stal-
   lone-net-worth.

7. Maxwell, John C., and Les Parrott, "Start with Your-
   self," in *25 Ways to Win With People: How to Make
   Others Feel Like a Million Bucks* (Nashville, TN: T.
   Nelson Publishers, 2005), 7–8.

ABOUT THE AUTHOR

K evin Templeton (Coach T.) has dedicated thirty-five years to working with high school and college-age young people in both the classroom and as a coach. Coach T. has coached basketball, baseball, and golf, and his teams have won numerous championships, including the 2003 NCCAA national basketball title. His experiences as well as his passion for kids and athletics have given him unique insight into what it takes to succeed on the court and in life. His use of humor and storytelling in this compilation of life lessons has become the core of his classroom leadership curriculum and focuses on character, choices, and friendships.

Coach T. is a character development coach and motivational speaker for high school students, college-age students, and athletic teams, providing seminars and even pregame speeches. He believes that telling a story is the best way to move a person's heart. *Nobody tells a story like Coach T.*